W9-AGC-521

A LITERARY READER

Latino
Writers
IN THE U.S.

nextext

Printed in the United States of America

ISBN 0-618-12055-6

6 7 8 9 — QVK — 05

Table of Contents

PART II: FAMILY

Throughout the reader, vocabulary words appear in boldface type and are footnoted. Specialized or technical words and phrases appear in lightface type and are footnoted.

The roots of Spanish speaking people in the United States date back to the colonial times, predating the arrival of the Mayflower. As a group they have been described in a variety of ways, among them, Spanish speakers, Hispanics, hispanos, and, more recently, Latinos. In this volume, we use the term "Latino" because it is more encompassing.

Authors' Roots

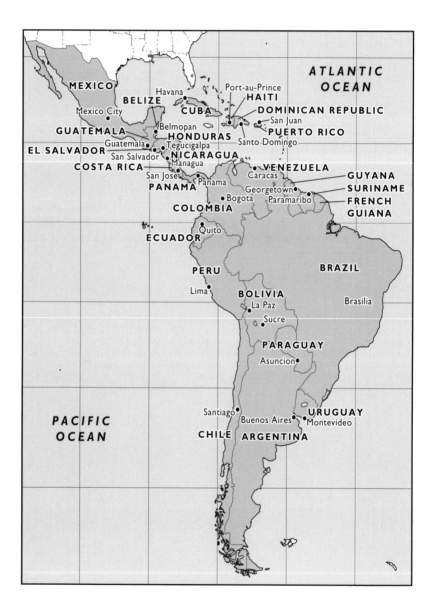

ATLANTIC OCEAN

MEXICO
Mexico City
BELIZE
Havana
Port-au-Prince
HAITI
CUBA
DOMINICAN REPUBLIC
San Juan
PUERTO RICO
GUATEMALA
Belmopan
HONDURAS
Guatemala
Tegucigalpa
Santo Domingo
EL SALVADOR
San Salvador
NICARAGUA
COSTA RICA
Managua
San Jose
VENEZUELA
Caracas
GUYANA
PANAMA
Panama
SURINAME
Georgetown
Paramaribo
FRENCH
Bogota
COLOMBIA
GUIANA
ECUADOR
Quito
PERU
BRAZIL
Lima
BOLIVIA
Brasilia
La Paz
Sucre
PARAGUAY
Asuncion
PACIFIC
OCEAN
Santiago
Buenos Aires
URUGUAY
Montevideo
CHILE
ARGENTINA

Traditions and Roots

Like Mexicans

BY GARY SOTO

Latino writers come out of cultural traditions that are intricate blendings of their families' native roots and experiences with U.S. society. Gary Soto was born in Fresno, California, in 1952 to parents of Mexican descent. He still lives in California. For many years he taught at the University of California, Berkeley. He has published nine poetry collections as well as books for young people, memoirs, and film scripts. His 1995 volume, New and Selected Poems, *was nominated for a National Book Award.*

My grandmother gave me bad advice and good advice when I was in my early teens. For the bad advice, she said that I should become a barber because they made good money and listened to the radio all day. "Honey, they don't work como burros,"[1] she would say every time I visited her. She made the sound of donkeys braying. "Like that, honey!" For the good

---

[1] como burros—like donkeys.

advice, she said that I should marry a Mexican girl. "No Okies, hijo"[2]—she would say—"Look my son. He marry one and they fight every day about I don't know what and I don't know what." For her, everyone who wasn't Mexican, black, or Asian were Okies. The French were Okies, the Italians in suits were Okies. When I asked about Jews, whom I had read about, she asked for a picture. I rode home on my bicycle and returned with a calendar depicting the important races of the world. "Pues sí, son Okies también!"[3] she said, nodding her head. She waved the calendar away and we went to the living room where she lectured me on the virtues of the Mexican girl: first, she could cook and, second, she acted like a woman, not a man, in her husband's home. She said she would tell me about a third when I got a little older.

I asked my mother about it—becoming a barber and marrying Mexican. She was in the kitchen. Steam curled from a pot of boiling beans, the radio was on, looking as squat as a loaf of bread. "Well, if you want to be a barber—they say they make good money." She slapped a round steak with a knife, her glasses slipping down with each strike. She stopped and looked up. "If you find a good Mexican girl, marry her of course." She returned to slapping the meat and I went to the backyard where my brother and David King were sitting on the lawn.

I ignored them and climbed the back fence to see my best friend, Scott, a second-generation Okie. I called him, and his mother pointed to the side of the house where his bedroom was a small aluminum trailer, the kind you gawk at when they're flipped over on the freeway, wheels spinning in the air. I went around to find Scott pitching horseshoes.

---

[2] "No Okies, hijo"—No Okies, son: *Okies* is a disrespectful term for people from Oklahoma.

[3] "Pues sí, son Okies también!"—Well yes, they're Okies, too!

I picked up a set of rusty ones and joined him. While we played, we talked about school and friends and record albums. The horseshoes scuffed up dirt, sometimes ringing the iron that threw out a meager[4] shadow like a sundial. After three argued-over games, we pulled two oranges apiece from his tree and started down the alley still talking school and friends and record albums. We pulled more oranges from the alley and talked about who we would marry. "No offense, Scott," I said with an orange slice in my mouth, "but I would never marry an Okie." We walked in step, almost touching. "No offense, Gary," Scott said, "but I would *never* marry a Mexican." I looked at him: a fang of orange slice showed from his munching mouth. I didn't think anything of it. He had his girl and I had mine. But our seventh-grade vision was the same: to marry, get jobs, buy cars and maybe a house if we had money left over.

We talked about our future lives until, to our surprise, we were on the downtown mall, two miles from home. We bought a bag of popcorn at Penney's and sat on a bench near the fountain watching Mexican and Okie girls pass. "That one's mine," I pointed with my chin when a girl with eyebrows arched into black rainbows ambled by. "She's cute," Scott said about a girl with yellow hair and a mouthful of gum. We dreamed aloud, our chins busy pointing out girls. We agreed that we couldn't wait to become men and lift them onto our laps.

But the woman I married was not Mexican but Japanese. It was a surprise to me. For years, I went about wide-eyed in my search for the brown girl in a white dress at a dance. I searched the playground at the baseball diamond. When the girls raced for grounders, their hair bounced like something that couldn't be

---

[4] **meager**—lean; weak.

caught. When they sat together in the lunchroom, heads pressed together, I knew they were talking about us Mexican guys. I saw them and dreamed them. I threw my face into my pillow, making up sentences that were good as in the movies.

But when I was twenty, I fell in love with this other girl who worried my mother, who had my grandmother asking once again to see the calendar of the Important Races of the World. I told her I had thrown it away years before. I took a much-glanced-at snapshot from my wallet. We looked at it together, in silence. Then grandma reclined in her chair, lit a cigarette, and said, "Es pretty."[5] She blew and asked with all her worry pushed up to her forehead: "Chinese?"

I was in love and there was no looking back. She was the one. I told my mother who was slapping hamburger into patties. "Well, sure if you want to marry her," she said. But the more I talked, the more concerned she became. Later I began to worry. Was it all a mistake? "Marry a Mexican girl," I heard my mother say in my mind. I heard it at breakfast. I heard it over math problems, between Western Civilization and cultural geography. But then one afternoon while I was hitchhiking home from school, it struck me like a baseball in the back: my mother wanted me to marry someone of my own social class—a poor girl. I considered my fiancée, Carolyn, and she didn't look poor, though I knew she came from a family of farm workers and pull-yourself-up-by-the-bootstraps ranchers. I asked my brother, who was marrying Mexican poor that fall, if I should marry a poor girl. He screamed "Yeah" above his terrible guitar playing in his bedroom. I considered my sister who had married Mexican. Cousins were dating Mexican. Uncles were remarrying poor women. I asked Scott, who was

[5] "Es pretty"—She's pretty.

still my best friend, and he said, "She's too good for you, so you better not."

I worried about it until Carolyn took me home to meet her parents. We drove in her Plymouth until the houses gave way to farms and ranches and finally her house fifty feet from the highway. When we pulled into the drive, I panicked and begged Carolyn to make a U-turn and go back so we could talk about it over a soda. She pinched my cheek, calling me a "silly boy." I felt better, though, when I got out of the car and saw the house: the chipped paint, a cracked window, boards for a walk to the back door. There were rusting cars near the barn. A tractor with a net of spiderwebs under a mulberry. A field. A bale of barbed wire like children's scribbling leaning against an empty chicken coop. Carolyn took my hand and pulled me to my future mother-in-law who was coming out to greet us.

We had lunch: sandwiches, potato chips, and iced tea. Carolyn and her mother talked mostly about neighbors and the congregation at the Japanese Methodist Church in West Fresno. Her father, who was in khaki work clothes, excused himself with a wave that was almost a salute and went outside. I heard a truck start, a dog bark, and then the truck rattle away.

Carolyn's mother offered another sandwich, but I declined with a shake of my head and a smile. I looked around when I could, when I was not saying over and over that I was a college student, hinting that I could take care of her daughter. I shifted my chair. I saw newspapers piled in corners, dusty cereal boxes and vinegar bottles in corners. The wallpaper was bubbled from rain that had come in from a bad roof. Dust. Dust lay on lamp shades and window sills. These people are just like Mexicans, I thought. Poor people.

Carolyn's mother asked me through Carolyn if I would like a *sushi*.[6] A plate of black and white things were held in front of me. I took one, wide-eyed, and turned it over like a foreign coin. I was biting into one when I saw a kitten crawl up the window screen over the sink. I chewed and the kitten opened its mouth in terror as she crawled higher, wanting in to paw the leftovers from our plates. I looked at Carolyn, who said that the cat was just showing off. I looked up in time to see it fall. It crawled up, then fell again.

We talked for an hour and had apple pie and coffee, slowly. Finally, we got up with Carolyn taking my hand. Slightly embarrassed, I tried to pull away but her grip held me. I let her have her way as she led me down the hallway with her mother right behind me. When I opened the door, I was startled by a kitten clinging to the screen door, its mouth screaming "cat food, dog biscuits, *sushi*. . . ." I opened the door and the kitten, still holding on, whined in the language of hungry animals. When I got into Carolyn's car, I looked back: the cat was still clinging. I asked Carolyn if it was possibly hungry, but she said the cat was being silly. She started the car, waved to her mother, and bounced us over the rain-pocked drive, patting my thigh for being her lover baby. Carolyn waved again. I looked back, waving, then gawking at a window screen where there were now three kittens clawing and screaming to get in. Like Mexicans, I thought. I remembered the Molinas and how the cats clung to their screens—cats they shot down with squirt guns. On the highway, I felt happy, pleased by it all. I patted Carolyn's thigh. Her people were like Mexicans, only different.

---

[6] *sushi*—Japanese dish of raw fish and rice.

QUESTIONS TO CONSIDER

1. What traditions do the speaker's relatives want him to carry on?

2. Why does the speaker feel better after his visit to Carolyn's house?

3. How do the speaker's interpretations of what "Mexicans" are like change over the years?

The Latin Deli: An Ars Poetica

BY JUDITH ORTÍZ COFER

The award-winning writer Judith Ortíz Cofer is the Franklin Professor of English and Creative Writing at the University of Georgia. She was born in Hormingueros, Puerto Rico, in 1952. Her books include a novel, The Line of the Sun, *two books of poetry,* Terms of Survival *and* Reaching for the Mainland, *and two collections of essays and poetry,* Silent Dancing *and* Of the Latin Deli: Prose and Poetry *(1995), from which the following poem comes.* Ars Poetica *in the title is Latin for "art of poetry." It refers to a work by the ancient Roman writer Horace and to any work that discusses poetry.*

Presiding over a formica counter,
plastic Mother and Child[1] magnetized
to the top of an ancient register,

---

[1] Mother and Child—images of Mary and the infant Jesus.

the heady mix of smells from the open bins
of dried codfish, the green plantains[2]
hanging in stalks like votive offerings,[3]
she is the Patroness of Exiles,
a woman of no-age who was never pretty,
who spends her days selling canned memories
while listening to the Puerto Ricans complain
that it would be cheaper to fly to San Juan
than to buy a pound of Bustelo coffee here,
and to Cubans perfecting their speech
of a "glorious return" to Havana—where no one
has been allowed to die and nothing to change
    until then;
to Mexicans who pass through, talking lyrically
of *dolares* to be made in El Norte—
all wanting the comfort
of spoken Spanish, to gaze upon the family portrait
of her plain wide face, her ample bosom
resting on her plump arms, her look of maternal interest
as they speak to her and each other
of their dreams and their disillusions—
how she smiles understanding,
when they walk down the narrow aisles of her store
reading the labels of packages aloud, as if
they were the names of lost lovers: *Suspiros,
Merengues,*[4] the stale candy of everyone's childhood.

---

[2] plantains—fruits of a large treelike plant. They look like bananas but are less
sweet and are a staple food of many South American and Asian cultures.

[3] votive offerings—presentations dedicated to gods.

[4] *Suspiros, Merengues*—sweet cookies.

She spends her days
slicing *jamon y queso* and wrapping it in wax paper
tied with string: plain ham and cheese
that would cost less at the A & P, but it would not satisfy
the hunger of the fragile old man lost in the folds
of his winter coat, who brings her lists of items
that he reads to her like poetry, or the others,
whose needs she must divine,[5] conjuring up products
from places that now exist only in their hearts—
closed ports she must trade with.

---

[5] divine—guess.

QUESTIONS TO CONSIDER

1. How is the woman at the deli counter like a family portrait?

2. What common traditions bring people into the deli?

3. How do the images used in the poem relate to the "Ars Poetica" of the title?

God Is Beside You on the Picketline

BY CESAR CHAVEZ

*Arguably the most important Latino activist in the United States,
Mexican-American labor organizer Cesar Chavez (1927–1993)
was the leading voice of Mexican Americans during the Civil Rights
era of the 1960s. His political quest is chronicled in* Sal Si Puedes:
Cesar Chavez and the New American Revolution *by Peter
Matthiessen. Chavez became a mythical figure among migrant
agricultural workers in the Southwest United States. His oratory
was down to earth. This speech was delivered in March 1966, in
the midst of a grape workers' strike. Chavez led a march from
Delano, California, to the state capital, Sacramento. A sign on
the union hall at Delano proclaimed: "God Is Beside You on the
Picketline." Most of the marchers were of the Roman Catholic
religious tradition. Chavez invokes religious images to inspire
political action.*

In the "March from Delano to Sacramento" there is a meeting of cultures and traditions; the centuries-old religious tradition of Spanish culture **conjoins**[1] with the very contemporary cultural syndrome of "demonstration" springing from the **spontaneity**[2] of the poor, the down-trodden, the rejected, the discriminated against bearing visibly their need and demand for equality and freedom.

In every religion-oriented culture "the pilgrimage" has had a place: a trip made with sacrifice and hardship as an expression of **penance**[3] and of commitment—and often involving a petition[4] to the patron of the pilgrim-age for some sincerely sought benefit of body or soul. Pilgrimage has not passed from Mexican culture. Daily at any of the major shrines of the country and in particular at the Basilica of the Lady of Guadalupe, there arrive pilgrims from all points—some of whom may have long since walked out the pieces of rubber tire that once served them as soles, and many of whom will walk on their knees the last mile or so of the pilgrimage. Many of the "pilgrims" of Delano will have walked such pilgrim-ages themselves in their lives—perhaps as very small children even—and cling to the memory of the day-long marches, the camps at night, streams forded, hills climbed, the sacral aura[5] of the sanctuary, and the "fiesta" that followed.

But throughout the Spanish-speaking world there is another tradition that touches the present march, that of the Lenten penitential processions, where the *penitentes* would march through the streets, often in sack cloth and ashes, some even carrying crosses, as a sign of penance for their sins, and as a plea for the mercy of God. The

---

[1] **conjoins**—unites.

[2] **spontaneity**—impulsiveness.

[3] **penance**—remorse; sorrow for sins.

[4] petition—solemn request.

[5] sacral aura—holy atmosphere.

penitential procession is also in the blood of the Mexican-American, and the Delano march will therefore be one of penance—public penance for the sins of the strikers, their own personal sins as well as their yielding perhaps to feelings of hatred and revenge in the strike itself. They hope by the march to set themselves at peace with the Lord, so that the justice of their cause will be purified of all lesser motivation.

These two great traditions of a great people meet in the Mexican-American with the belief that Delano is his "cause," his great demand for justice, freedom, and respect from a **predominantly**[6] foreign cultural community in a land where he was first. The revolutions of Mexico were primarily uprisings of the poor, fighting for bread and for dignity. The Mexican-American is also a child of the revolution.

Pilgrimage, penance, and revolution. The pilgrimage from Delano to Sacramento has strong religio-cultural overtones. But it is also the pilgrimage of a cultural minority which has suffered from a hostile environment, and a minority which means business.

---

[6] **predominantly**—more powerful.

QUESTIONS TO CONSIDER

1. How is a protest march similar to and different from the religious traditions Chavez describes?

2. According to Chavez, for what might the marchers be penitent?

3. According to Chavez, how will the march help the marchers?

from

Bless Me, Ultima

BY RUDOLFO A. ANAYA

Rudolfo Anaya was born in 1937 in Pastura, New Mexico, and taught for some time at the University of New Mexico. In 1972, his novel Bless Me, Ultima, *about a young boy's shifting perspective on his family's traditions, was published and won the Premio Quinto Sol literary award. Anaya has more than two dozen titles to his credit, including* Tortuga, *about a boy who must live in a body cast,* A Chicano in China, *which won the Before Columbus Foundation American Book Award, and* Alburquerque.

Ultima came to stay with us the summer I was almost seven. When she came the beauty of the llano[1] unfolded before my eyes, and the gurgling waters of the river sang to the hum of the turning earth. The magical time of childhood stood still, and the pulse of the living earth pressed its mystery into my living blood. She took my hand, and the silent, magic powers she possessed

---

[1] llano—large, grassy, almost treeless plain.

made beauty from the raw, sun-baked llano, the green river valley, and the blue bowl which was the white sun's home. My bare feet felt the throbbing earth and my body trembled with excitement. Time stood still, and it shared with me all that had been, and all that was to come. . . .

Let me begin at the beginning. I do not mean the beginning that was in my dreams and the stories they whispered to me about my birth, and the people of my father and mother, and my three brothers—but the beginning that came with Ultima.

The attic of our home was partitioned into two small rooms. My sisters, Deborah and Theresa, slept in one and I slept in the small cubicle by the door. The wooden steps creaked down into a small hallway that led into the kitchen. From the top of the stairs I had a vantage point into the heart of our home, my mother's kitchen. From there I was to see the terrified face of Chávez when he brought the terrible news of the murder of the sheriff; I was to see the rebellion of my brothers against my father; and many times late at night I was to see Ultima returning from the llano where she gathered the herbs that can be harvested only in the light of the full moon by the careful hands of a curandera.[2]

That night I lay very quietly in my bed, and I heard my father and mother speak of Ultima.

"Está sola," my father said, "ya no queda gente en el pueblito de Las Pasturas—"[3]

He spoke in Spanish, and the village he mentioned was his home. My father had been a vaquero[4] all his life, a calling as ancient as the coming of the Spaniard to Nuevo Méjico.[5] Even after the big rancheros and the

---

[2] curandera—healing woman.

[3] "Está sola. . . Las Pasturas"—She's alone now that there's no one living in the little town of Las Pasturas.

[4] vaquero—cowboy.

[5] Nuevo Méjico—New Mexico.

tejanos[6] came and fenced the beautiful llano, he and those like him continued to work there, I guess because only in that wide expanse of land and sky could they feel the freedom their spirits needed.

"¡Qué lástima!"[7] my mother answered, and I knew her nimble fingers worked the pattern on the doily she crocheted for the big chair in the sala.[8]

I heard her sigh, and she must have shuddered too when she thought of Ultima living alone in the loneliness of the wide llano. My mother was not a woman of the llano, she was the daughter of a farmer. She could not see beauty in the llano and she could not understand the coarse men who lived half their lifetimes on horseback. After I was born in Las Pasturas she persuaded my father to leave the llano and bring her family to the town of Guadalupe where she said there would be opportunity and school for us. The move lowered my father in the esteem of his compadres,[9] the other vaqueros of the llano who clung **tenaciously**[10] to their way of life and freedom. There was no room to keep animals in town so my father had to sell his small herd, but he would not sell his horse so he gave it to a good friend, Benito Campos. But Campos could not keep the animal penned up because somehow the horse was very close to the spirit of the man, and so the horse was allowed to roam free and no vaquero on that llano would throw a lazo[11] on that horse. It was as if someone had died, and they turned their gaze from the spirit that walked the earth.

It hurt my father's pride. He saw less and less of his old compadres. He went to work on the highway and on Saturdays after they collected their pay he drank with

---

[6] tejanos—Texans.

[7] "¡Qué lástima!"—What a pity!

[8] sala—living room.

[9] compadres—buddies.

[10] **tenaciously**—stubbornly.

[11] lazo—lasso (rope).

his crew at the Longhorn, but he was never close to the men of the town. Some weekends the llaneros[12] would come into town for supplies and old amigos[13] like Bonney or Campos or the Gonzales brothers would come by to visit. Then my father's eyes lit up as they drank and talked of the old days and told the old stories. But when the western sun touched the clouds with orange and gold the vaqueros got in their trucks and headed home, and my father was left to drink alone in the long night. Sunday morning he would get up very crudo[14] and complain about having to go to early mass.

"—She served the people all her life, and now the people are scattered, driven like tumbleweeds by the winds of war. The war sucks everything dry," my father said solemnly, "it takes the young boys overseas, and their families move to California where there is work—"

"Ave María Purísima," my mother made the sign of the cross for my three brothers who were away at war. "Gabriel," she said to my father, "it is not right that la Grande be alone in her old age—"

"No," my father agreed.

"When I married you and went to the llano to live with you and raise your family, I could not have survived without la Grande's help. Oh, those were hard years—"

"Those were good years," my father countered. But my mother would not argue.

"There isn't a family she did not help," she continued, "no road was too long for her to walk to its end to snatch somebody from the jaws of death, and not even the blizzards of the llano could keep her from the appointed place where a baby was to be delivered—"

"Es verdad,"[15] my father nodded.

---

[12] llaneros—plainsmen.

[13] amigos—friends.

[14] crudo—hung over.

[15] "Es verdad"—It is true.

"She tended me at the birth of my sons—" And then I knew her eyes glanced briefly at my father. "Gabriel, we cannot let her live her last days in loneliness—"

"No," my father agreed, "it is not the way of our people."

"It would be a great honor to provide a home for la Grande," my mother murmured. My mother called Ultima la Grande out of respect. It meant the woman was old and wise.

"I have already sent word with Campos that Ultima is to come and live with us," my father said with some satisfaction. He knew it would please my mother.

"I am grateful," my mother said tenderly, "perhaps we can repay a little of the kindness la Grande has given to so many."

"And the children?" my father asked. I knew why he expressed concern for me and my sisters. It was because Ultima was a curandera, a woman who knew the herbs and remedies of the ancients, a miracle-worker who could heal the sick. And I had heard that Ultima could lift the curses laid by brujas,[16] that she could **exorcise**[17] the evil the witches planted in people to make them sick. And because a curandera had this power she was misunderstood and often suspected of practicing witchcraft herself.

I shuddered and my heart turned cold at the thought. The cuentos[18] of the people were full of the tales of evil done by brujas.

"She helped bring them into the world, she cannot be but good for the children," my mother answered.

"Está bien,"[19] my father yawned, "I will go for her in the morning."

---

[16] brujas—witches.

[17] **exorcise**—expel; cast out.

[18] cuentos—stories.

[19] "Está bien"—She is good.

So it was decided that Ultima should come and live with us. I knew that my father and mother did good by providing a home for Ultima. It was the custom to provide for the old and the sick. There was always room in the safety and warmth of la familia for one more person, be that person stranger or friend.

It was warm in the attic, and as I lay quietly listening to the sounds of the house falling asleep and repeating a Hail Mary[20] over and over in my thoughts, I drifted into the time of dreams. Once I had told my mother about my dreams, and she said they were visions from God and she was happy, because her own dream was that I should grow up and become a priest. After that I did not tell her about my dreams, and they remained in me forever and ever . . .

In my dream I flew over the rolling hills of the llano. My soul wandered over the dark plain until it came to a cluster of adobe huts. I recognized the village of Las Pasturas and my heart grew happy. One mud hut had a lighted window, and the vision of my dream swept me towards it to be witness at the birth of a baby.

I could not make out the face of the mother who rested from the pains of birth, but I could see the old woman in black who tended the just-arrived, steaming baby. She nimbly tied a knot on the cord that had connected the baby to its mother's blood, then quickly she bent and with her teeth she bit off the loose end. She wrapped the squirming baby and laid it at the mother's side, then she returned to cleaning the bed. All linen was swept aside to be washed, but she carefully wrapped the useless cord and the afterbirth and laid the package at the feet of the Virgin on the small altar. I sensed that these things were yet to be delivered to someone.

Now the people who had waited patiently in the dark were allowed to come in and speak to the mother and deliver their gifts to the baby. I recognized my mother's brothers, my uncles

---

[20] Hail Mary—prayer to the mother of Jesus.

from El Puerto de los Lunas. They entered ceremoniously. A patient hope stirred in their dark, brooding eyes.

This one will be a Luna, the old man said, he will be a farmer and keep our customs and traditions. Perhaps God will bless our family and make the baby a priest.

And to show their hope they rubbed the dark earth of the river valley on the baby's forehead, and they surrounded the bed with the fruits of their harvest so the small room smelled of fresh green chile and corn, ripe apples and peaches, pumpkins and green beans.

Then the silence was shattered with the thunder of hoof-beats; vaqueros surrounded the small house with shouts and gunshots, and when they entered the room they were laughing and singing and drinking.

Gabriel, they shouted, you have a fine son! He will make a fine vaquero! And they smashed the fruits and vegetables that surrounded the bed and replaced them with a saddle, horse blankets, bottles of whiskey, a new rope, bridles, chapas,[21] and an old guitar. And they rubbed the stain of earth from the baby's forehead because man was not to be tied to the earth but free upon it.

These were the people of my father, the vaqueros of the llano. They were an **exuberant**,[22] *restless people, wandering across the ocean of the plain.*

We must return to our valley, the old man who led the farmers spoke. We must take with us the blood that comes after the birth. We will bury it in our fields to renew their fertility and to assure that the baby will follow our ways. He nodded for the old woman to deliver the package at the altar.

No! the llaneros protested, it will stay here! We will burn it and let the winds of the llano scatter the ashes.

It is **blasphemy**[23] *to scatter a man's blood on unholy ground, the farmers chanted. The new son must fulfill his*

---

[21] *chapas*—a coin-tossing game.

[22] **exuberant**—high-spirited.

[23] **blasphemy**—disrespect toward God.

mother's dream. He must come to El Puerto and rule over the Lunas of the valley. The blood of the Lunas is strong in him.

He is a Márez, the vaqueros shouted. His forefathers were conquistadores, men as restless as the seas they sailed and as free as the land they conquered. He is his father's blood!

Curses and threats filled the air, pistols were drawn, and the opposing sides made ready for battle. But the clash was stopped by the old woman who delivered the baby.

Cease! she cried, and the men were quiet. I pulled this baby into the light of life, so I will bury the afterbirth and the cord that once linked him to eternity. Only I will know his destiny.

The dream began to dissolve. When I opened my eyes I heard my father cranking the truck outside. I wanted to go with him, I wanted to see Las Pasturas, I wanted to see Ultima. I dressed hurriedly, but I was too late. The truck was bouncing down the goat path that led to the bridge and the highway.

I turned, as I always did, and looked down the slope of our hill to the green of the river, and I raised my eyes and saw the town of Guadalupe. Towering above the housetops and the trees of the town was the church tower. I made the sign of the cross on my lips. The only other building that rose above the housetops to compete with the church tower was the yellow top of the schoolhouse. This fall I would be going to school.

My heart sank. When I thought of leaving my mother and going to school a warm, sick feeling came to my stomach. To get rid of it I ran to the pens we kept by the molino[24] to feed the animals. I had fed the rabbits that night and they still had alfalfa and so I only changed their water. I scattered some grain for the hungry chickens and watched their mad scramble as the rooster called them to peck. I milked the cow and turned her loose. During the day she would **forage**[25] along the highway

---

[24] molino—mill.

[25] **forage**—search for food.

where the grass was thick and green, then she would return at nightfall. She was a good cow and there were very few times when I had to run and bring her back in the evening. Then I dreaded it, because she might wander into the hills where the bats flew at dusk and there was only the sound of my heart beating as I ran and it made me sad and frightened to be alone.

I collected three eggs in the chicken house and returned for breakfast.

"Antonio," my mother smiled and took the eggs and milk, "come and eat your breakfast."

I sat across the table from Deborah and Theresa and ate my atole[26] and the hot tortilla with butter. I said very little. I usually spoke very little to my two sisters. They were older than I and they were very close. They usually spent the entire day in the attic, playing dolls and giggling. I did not concern myself with those things.

"Your father has gone to Las Pasturas," my mother chattered, "he has gone to bring la Grande." Her hands were white with the flour of the dough. I watched carefully. "—And when he returns, I want you children to show your manners. You must not shame your father or your mother—"

"Isn't her real name Ultima?" Deborah asked. She was like that, always asking grown-up questions.

"You will address her as la Grande," my mother said flatly. I looked at her and wondered if this woman with the black hair and laughing eyes was the woman who gave birth in my dream.

"Grande," Theresa repeated.

"Is it true she is a witch?" Deborah asked. Oh, she was in for it. I saw my mother whirl then pause and control herself.

"No!" she scolded. "You must not speak of such things! Oh, I don't know where you learn such ways—"

---

[26] atole—cooked corn meal.

Her eyes flooded with tears. She always cried when she thought we were learning the ways of my father, the ways of the Márez. "She is a woman of learning," she went on and I knew she didn't have time to stop and cry, "she has worked hard for all the people of the village. Oh, I would never have survived those hard years if it had not been for her—so show her respect. We are honored that she comes to live with us, understand?"

"Sí, mamá," Deborah said half willingly.

"Sí, mamá," Theresa repeated.

"Now run and sweep the room at the end of the hall. Eugene's room—" I heard her voice choke. She breathed a prayer and crossed her forehead. The flour left white stains on her, the four points of the cross. I knew it was because my three brothers were at war that she was sad, and Eugene was the youngest.

"Mamá." I wanted to speak to her. I wanted to know who the old woman was who cut the baby's cord.

"Sí." She turned and looked at me.

"Was Ultima at my birth?" I asked.

"¡Ay Dios mío!"[27] my mother cried. She came to where I sat and ran her hand through my hair. She smelled warm, like bread. "Where do you get such questions, my son. Yes," she smiled, "la Grande was there to help me. She was there to help at the birth of all of my children—"

"And my uncles from El Puerto were there?"

"Of course," she answered, "my brothers have always been at my side when I needed them. They have always prayed that I would bless them with a—"

I did not hear what she said because I was hearing the sounds of the dream, and I was seeing the dream again. The warm cereal in my stomach made me feel sick.

"And my father's brother was there, the Márez' and their friends, the vaqueros—"

---

[27] "¡Ay Dios mío!"—Oh my God!

"Ay!" she cried out, "Don't speak to me of those worthless Márez and their friends!"

"There was a fight?" I asked.

"No," she said, "a silly argument. They wanted to start a fight with my brothers—that is all they are good for. Vaqueros, they call themselves, they are worthless drunks! Thieves! Always on the move, like gypsies, always dragging their families around the country like vagabonds—"

As long as I could remember she always raged about the Márez family and their friends. She called the village of Las Pasturas beautiful; she had gotten used to the loneliness, but she had never accepted its people. She was the daughter of farmers.

But the dream was true. It was as I had seen it. Ultima knew.

"But you will not be like them." She caught her breath and stopped. She kissed my forehead. "You will be like my brothers. You will be a Luna, Antonio. You will be a man of the people, and perhaps a priest." She smiled.

A priest, I thought, that was her dream. I was to hold mass on Sundays like Father Byrnes did in the church in town. I was to hear the confessions of the silent people of the valley, and I was to administer the holy Sacrament to them.

"Perhaps," I said.

"Yes," my mother smiled. She held me tenderly. The fragrance of her body was sweet.

"But then," I whispered, "who will hear my confession?"[28]

"What?"

"Nothing," I answered. I felt a cool sweat on my forehead and I knew I had to run, I had to clear my mind of the dream. "I am going to Jasón's house," I said

---

[28] confession—telling of sins in the religious rite of admitting wrongs and asking forgiveness.

hurriedly and slid past my mother. I ran out the kitchen door, past the animal pens, towards Jasón's house. The white sun and the fresh air cleansed me.

On this side of the river there were only three houses. The slope of the hill rose gradually into the hills of juniper and mesquite and cedar[29] clumps. Jasón's house was farther away from the river than our house. On the path that led to the bridge lived huge, fat Fío and his beautiful wife. Fío and my father worked together on the highway. They were good drinking friends.

"¡Jasón!" I called at the kitchen door. I had run hard and was panting. His mother appeared at the door.

"Jasón no está aquí,"[30] she said. All of the older people spoke only in Spanish, and I myself understood only Spanish. It was only after one went to school that one learned English.

"¿Dónde está?"[31] I asked.

She pointed towards the river, northwest, past the railroad tracks to the dark hills. The river came through those hills and there were old Indian grounds there, holy burial grounds Jasón told me. There in an old cave lived his Indian. At least everybody called him Jasón's Indian. He was the only Indian of the town, and he talked only to Jasón. Jasón's father had forbidden Jasón to talk to the Indian, he had beaten him, he had tried in every way to keep Jasón from the Indian.

But Jasón persisted. Jasón was not a bad boy, he was just Jasón. He was quiet and moody, and sometimes for no reason at all wild, loud sounds came exploding from his throat and lungs. Sometimes I felt like Jasón, like I wanted to shout and cry, but I never did.

I looked at his mother's eyes and I saw they were sad. "Thank you," I said, and returned home. While I waited for my father to return with Ultima I worked in

---

[29] juniper, mesquite, cedar—fragrant trees and shrubs native to dry regions.

[30] "Jasón no está aquí"—Jason isn't here.

[31] "¿Dónde está?"—Where is he?

the garden. Every day I had to work in the garden. Every day I reclaimed from the rocky soil of the hill a few more feet of earth to cultivate. The land of the llano was not good for farming, the good land was along the river. But my mother wanted a garden and I worked to make her happy. Already we had a few chile and tomato plants growing. It was hard work. My fingers bled from scraping out the rocks and it seemed that a square yard of ground produced a wheelbarrow full of rocks which I had to push down to the retaining wall.

The sun was white in the bright blue sky. The shade of the clouds would not come until the afternoon. The sweat was sticky on my brown body. I heard the truck and turned to see it chugging up the dusty goat path. My father was returning with Ultima.

"¡Mamá!" I called. My mother came running out, Deborah and Theresa trailed after her.

"I'm afraid," I heard Theresa whimper.

"There's nothing to be afraid of," Deborah said confidently. My mother said there was too much Márez blood in Deborah. Her eyes and hair were very dark, and she was always running. She had been to school two years and she spoke only English. She was teaching Theresa, and half the time I didn't understand what they were saying.

"Madre de Dios,[32] but mind your manners!" my mother scolded. The truck stopped and she ran to greet Ultima. "Buenos días le de Dios,[33] Grande," my mother cried. She smiled and hugged and kissed the old woman.

"Ay, María Luna," Ultima smiled, "Buenos días te de Dios, a ti y a tu familia."[34] She wrapped the black shawl around her hair and shoulders. Her face was brown and

---

[32] "Madre de Dios"—Mother of God.

[33] "Buenos días le de Dios"—Good day of the lord.

[34] "Buenos días te de Dios, a ti y a tu familia"—Good day of the lord to you and your family.

very wrinkled. When she smiled her teeth were brown. I remembered the dream.

"Come, come!" my mother urged us forward. It was the custom to greet the old. "Deborah!" my mother urged. Deborah stepped forward and took Ultima's withered hand.

"Buenos días, Grande," she smiled. She even bowed slightly. Then she pulled Theresa forward and told her to greet la Grande. My mother beamed. Deborah's good manners surprised her, but they made her happy, because a family was judged by its manners.

"What beautiful daughters you have raised," Ultima nodded to my mother. Nothing could have pleased my mother more. She looked proudly at my father who stood leaning against the truck, watching and judging the introductions.

"Antonio," he said simply. I stepped forward and took Ultima's hand. I looked up into her clear brown eyes and shivered. Her face was old and wrinkled, but her eyes were clear and sparkling, like the eyes of a young child.

"Antonio,"' she smiled. She took my hand and I felt the power of a whirlwind sweep around me. Her eyes swept the surrounding hills and through them I saw for the first time the wild beauty of our hills and the magic of the green river. My nostrils quivered as I felt the song of the mockingbirds and the drone of the grasshoppers mingle with the pulse of the earth. The four directions of the llano met in me, and the white sun shone on my soul. The granules of sand at my feet and the sun and sky above me seemed to dissolve into one strange, complete being.

A cry came to my throat, and I wanted to shout it and run in the beauty I had found.

"Antonio." I felt my mother prod me. Deborah giggled because she had made the right greeting, and I who was to be my mother's hope and joy stood voiceless.

"Buenos días le de Dios, Ultima," I muttered. I saw in her eyes my dream. I saw the old woman who had delivered me from my mother's womb. I knew she held the secret of my destiny.

"¡Antonio!" My mother was shocked I had used her name instead of calling her Grande. But Ultima held up her hand.

"Let it be," she smiled, "This was the last child I pulled from your womb, María. I knew there would be something between us."

My mother who had started to mumble apologies was quiet. "As you wish, Grande," she nodded.

"I have come to spend the last days of my life here, Antonio," Ultima said to me.

"You will never die, Ultima," I answered, "I will take care of you—" She let go of my hand and laughed. Then my father said, "pase, Grande, pase. Nuestra casa es su casa.[35] It is too hot to stand and visit in the sun—"

"Sí, sí," my mother urged. I watched them go in. My father carried on his shoulders the large blue-tin trunk which later I learned contained all of Ultima's earthly possessions, the black dresses and shawls she wore, and the magic of her sweet smelling herbs.

As Ultima walked past me I smelled for the first time a trace of the sweet fragrance of herbs that always lingered in her wake. Many years later, long after Ultima was gone and I had grown to be a man, I would awaken sometimes at night and think I caught a scent of her fragrance in the cool-night breeze.

And with Ultima came the owl. I heard it that night for the first time in the juniper tree outside of Ultima's window. I knew it was her owl because the other owls of the llano did not come that near the house. At first it disturbed me, and Deborah and Theresa too. I heard

---

[35] "pase, Grande, pase. Nuestra casa es su casa"—enter, enter. Our home is your home.

them whispering through the partition. I heard Deborah reassuring Theresa that she would take care of her, and then she took Theresa in her arms and rocked her until they were both asleep.

I waited. I was sure my father would get up and shoot the owl with the old rifle he kept on the kitchen wall. But he didn't, and I accepted his understanding. In many cuentos I had heard the owl was one of the disguises a bruja took, and so it struck a chord of fear in the heart to hear them hooting at night. But not Ultima's owl. Its soft hooting was like a song, and as it grew rhythmic it calmed the moonlit hills and lulled us to sleep. Its song seemed to say that it had come to watch over us.

I dreamed about the owl that night, and my dream was good. La Virgen de Guadalupe was the patron saint of our town. The town was named after her. In my dream I saw Ultima's owl lift la Virgen on her wide wings and fly her to heaven. Then the owl returned and gathered up all the babes of Limbo[36] and flew them up to the clouds of heaven.

The Virgin smiled at the goodness of the owl.

---

[36] Limbo—in Roman Catholic tradition, a place for babies who are barred from heaven because they have not been baptized.

QUESTIONS TO CONSIDER

1. What traditions make it possible for Ultima to come live with the speaker's family?

2. How do traditions come into conflict with each other in this story?

3. How do his parents' family backgrounds influence the speaker's thoughts and feelings?

Mrs. Vargas and the Dead Naturalist

BY KATHLEEN ALCALÁ

A novelist interested in women's history, Kathleen Alcalá was born in California in 1954 of Mexican parents and now lives in Washington state. She is the author of several novels, including Spirit of the Ordinary. *She has won the Pacific Northwest Bookseller's Award and the Western States Book Award for Fiction. One of her favorite themes is the life of crypto-Jews in Mexico. These are descendents of Jews who fled Spain to escape being persecuted by the Roman Catholic Inquisition of the 1400s. This story comes from Alcalá's acclaimed 1992 collection of the same title.*

Mrs. Vargas had been cleaning the house for a week in anticipation of the visit, and the guest wasn't due for at least three more days. The hemp floormats had been beaten and aired out, the whitewashed walls had been scrubbed inside and out, and Mrs. Vargas was now spreading her best embroidered tablecloth on the big square table in the sala while admonishing her family not to spill anything on it for the next few days. When she heard the thump on the door, she thought it was a neighbor.

"*¡Entren!*"[1] she said loudly. Mrs. Vargas, a short, sturdy woman, fluttered her hands over her hair as she started towards the door. The handle turned, and a dusty figure half-walked, half-fell into the front room. She had never seen him before.

"Dr. Ellis?" she said, "Dr. Ellis?" Receiving no answer, she helped him to a wicker chair. The Anglo was greenish-white, and a cold sweat stood on his forehead and upper lip. Panting heavily, he said nothing, but looked up at her with pleading eyes.

"*¡Agua!*"[2] she yelled. "Just a minute, I'll bring you some water." And she patted him into the chair as though that would keep him from falling over while she went for cold water. Returning from the kitchen with her daughter, she could see that it was too late. He was slumped over and not breathing.

Nevertheless, she said, "Luz, go get the *curandera*, and you," she said to her other children, attracted by the commotion, "help me put him on the bed." A leather folder fell to the floor as they carried the dusty man to the guest bedroom and laid his body on the clean cotton bedspread.

As she had suspected, the **naturalist**[3] was quite dead by the time help arrived.

"It was his heart," said the *curandera*. "Besides, he drank too much. That's why he's so yellow."

The man looked older than Mrs. Vargas had imagined, and was not well dressed. He wore a torn black raincoat completely unsuited to the Yucatec[4] climate, a cheap cotton shirt, and polyester pants that were frayed at the cuffs. He wasn't at all what she had expected.

---

[1] "*¡Entren!*"—Come in!

[2] "*¡Agua!*"—Water!

[3] **naturalist**—person who studies animals and plants.

[4] Yucatec—of a state in southeastern Mexico, whose capital is Mérida.

"Dear Claudia," the letter from her sister in Mérida had begun. "I have a favor to ask of you. A man my husband sometimes works for, a famous naturalist, would like to go to our village to study the *ikeek*, which the Americans call the 'rockbird.' Since there is no place to stay, I thought you might be able to accommodate him for a few days. I am sure that he would be very appreciative of the favor. Please let me know if this will be all right." Mrs. Vargas had quickly written back, mindful of the **prestige**[5] which might result from having a famous naturalist as her guest in the village.

As the *curandera* was finishing up, the priest arrived.

"What happened?" he asked.

"He had a heart attack and died," said Mrs. Vargas. "I guess the journey was too much for him."

"Is it the scientist?" he asked.

"Well, he's an American. Who else would it be?" Then Mrs. Vargas remembered the portfolio. Finding it on the floor, she and the priest unzipped its stiff edges and looked inside. It contained colored pencils and drawings of tropical birds on very thin paper.

"But how did he get here?" asked the priest. "The bus doesn't come this far. And where is his luggage? His passport?" No one knew the answers to these questions. By now, a crowd had gathered outside.

"We saw him walking up the road," said Saladino Chan, "as we were returning from the fields. He asked the way to Mrs. Vargas' house. He didn't have any luggage then, and he didn't look well."

"Maybe he walked from Napual, where the bus stops, and forgot his suitcase. Or maybe he was robbed." Yes, nodded everyone, or maybe he was having it sent later, with special scientific equipment. In any case, it would be of no help to him now.

---

[5] **prestige**—distinction.

Mrs. Vargas perched on a chair for a minute to collect her thoughts. She was upset by the death, but at the same time, the prone figure[6] in the bedroom filled her with uneasiness. She wasn't sure just what sort of a guest he would have been, anyway.

After administering the last rites to Dr. Ellis, the priest returned to the front room and sat down opposite Mrs. Vargas. "We could take the body by truck to Napual, and put it on the bus back to Mérida," said the priest, "but it is very hot, and I'm afraid the body will deteriorate. I think we should bury him here."

"Yes—" said Mrs. Vargas, perking up a little, "at least we can give him a nice funeral."

So a black wooden coffin was prepared for the naturalist, and the stonemason carved his name on a slab of marble he'd been saving for something special. The next morning, the coffin was covered with the bright flowers of the hyacinth and the blossoms of the silkcotton tree. The coffin bearers sang the songs for the dead as they marched in procession to the cemetery, and the whole village turned out for the occasion.

"God respects those who respect his creations, and scientists who study birds and flowers, in their own way, respect and conserve God's work," said the priest. The people nodded, final prayers were said, and the coffin was lowered into the rocky grave. Everyone gave their **condolences**[7] to Mrs. Vargas, since the naturalist had no family present.

After that, the men went off to the fields, and everyone agreed that it was the best funeral they'd had in a while. The bill for the headstone would be sent to the university.

Mrs. Vargas, still crying a little, hurried home to write to her sister and tell her the bad news. The cotton bedspread was washed, and her three younger boys,

---

[6] prone figure—person lying face down.

[7] **condolences**—expressions of sympathy.

who had been sent to stay with cousins, moved back into the guest bedroom.

Three days later, a Toyota Land Cruiser roared into the village. An American asked directions to Mrs. Vargas' house, and drove on.

"It must be someone from the American consulate," said the villagers, finding an excuse to walk up the road that led to Mrs. Vargas' house.

The Land Cruiser stopped in front, and out jumped a trim, athletic man in his mid-thirties. He was not dressed like a diplomat, but instead wore a khaki shirt and trousers.

"Mrs. Vargas?" he asked, when she opened the door. "I'm Dr. Ellis, from the university," and he smiled his best American smile.

An expression between horror and ecstasy[8] crossed her face and, with a little cry, Mrs. Vargas swooned into her daughter's arms. Luz, confused and scared, burst into tears while the naturalist stood in the doorway, unsure whether to try and help, shifting the strap to his expensive camera uncomfortably on his shoulder.

Finally, Mrs. Vargas blinked her eyes and, assuring the man that she was all right, offered him a chair and described the death of a few days before.

"What did he look like?" asked Dr. Ellis.

"An older man with yellow skin," she said, "and a black raincoat. He carried a leather envelope with pictures of birds."

"How strange," said Ellis. "I have no idea who that could have been. Didn't he have a passport or anything?"

"No," said Mrs. Vargas. "We found nothing in his pockets, and he had no luggage. All he brought were the drawings."

At her mother's bidding, Luz brought out the worn portfolio, and Ellis opened it. He carefully examined the

---

[8] **ecstasy**—delight.

drawings, which were unsigned, and turned the folder inside out looking for clues, but there was nothing. The colored pencils had been manufactured in Mexico, and were the sort commonly used by schoolchildren.

"I don't know what to tell you," said Ellis, "except that people sometimes write to the university, or call, if they think they've seen something unusual. He might have called after I left and found out I'd be here. But I don't know anything about him. I'm sorry."

Mrs. Vargas recalled the **acrid**[9] smell of the dead man's skin, and her sense of foreboding returned. "I thought there was something odd about him. He didn't look right."

"I'm very sorry about the mixup," said Dr. Ellis. "If I can compensate you, or someone, for the burial expenses, I would like to do that. I guess someone should notify the authorities, if it hasn't been done. I would be happy to take care of it."

He waited for a response from Mrs. Vargas, who sat with her hands folded in her lap. She seemed to have forgotten him.

"Oh, yes," she said finally. "I'm sure it can be worked out." She realized that the young scientist was waiting to be invited to remain. "If the circumstances permit, I hope that you will stay and continue with your work."

"If that's all right," he answered. "After all the confusion, I hope it's not too much trouble."

"Not at all," she answered. "My house is your house."

So the three younger boys went out the back door to their cousins' again, while Dr. Ellis brought his suitcase and several six-packs of Orange Crush in the front door. He opened and gave a bottle to each of the remaining

---

[9] **acrid**—bitter.

children, and they drank the warm soda right before dinner, much to Mrs. Vargas' **consternation**,[10] but she said nothing.

At dinner, on the old tablecloth, since the good one had been soiled in the meantime, Dr. Ellis gave her a fancy silver salt and pepper set.

"I thought you might like these," he said. She thanked him profusely and placed them out on the table. She didn't tell him that she would never use them, since the high humidity made salt stick together, and it would clog up the little holes in the shaker.

Dr. Ellis told them about his work. He taught ornithology[11] at the university and studied the birds of southern Mexico and Guatemala. The rockbird was of interest because it is one of the few species of birds which maintains a *lek,* or dancing ground, which the male clears on the jungle floor in order to display his beautiful feathers and attract a mate.

"The reported sightings near your village," continued Dr. Ellis, "if confirmed, would make this the farthest north this type of bird has ever been found in the Americas. It would change the maps of ornithology!" The family nodded politely and ate their beans and tortillas. They didn't tell him that he would sleep that night where the dead man had lain.

The next morning, Dr. Ellis set out early to find the rockbird. Overtaking some farmers on the way to their fields, he asked if they had seen the small yellow bird.

"Oh, yes," they said nervously, "it has been seen. Out there. It lives out in the jungle." But no one seemed to know just where.

Late that afternoon, on his way back to the village, Ellis stopped by the cemetery to pay his respects, and saw the tombstone with his own name on it. He went

---

[10] **consternation**—great dismay.

[11] ornithology—science of birds.

into town to the cantina,[12] found the stonemason, and offered to pay for the tombstone, if he would just take it down. After a few beers, and after **ascertaining**[13] that the real occupant of the grave was penniless and unknown, the mason decided to reuse the stone on another occasion, and would put up a wooden cross instead. He was very grateful for the handsome pen and pencil set which the scientist gave to him.

Ellis noticed that, as he walked down the street, people shrank back to let him pass, and were careful not to let even their clothing touch him. Whispers followed him, and a few of the older women even crossed themselves. The next morning, walking out to the jungle with the farmers, he saw that the headstone with his name on it had been taken down, and additional, plain stones had been piled onto the already mounded grave.

"Why are there more stones on the grave?" he asked.

"Just to make sure," was the answer.

Again, he searched fruitlessly for any sign of the rockbird. The drawings in the portfolio had included one of a yellow bird, but it looked more like a glorified canary than anything else. Ellis suspected that it had been traced from another picture. Again, that evening, he asked the villagers if they had ever seen the bird, and instead of specific answers, received only vague, affirmative answers.

Finally, the *curandera* said to him, "We only see the *ikeek,* as we call it, when someone in the village is about to die. The bird waits to accompany the spirit back to the gates of heaven, so that it won't get lost."

After that, Ellis stopped asking the villagers for help, but continued to search the jungles on his own for two more days. He found a single yellow feather that could have belonged to any bird at all, but he took a picture of

---

[12] cantina—tavern.

[13] **ascertaining**—making sure.

it, wrote down the location, and sealed it up in a little plastic envelope for further analysis.

Disappointed by his lack of findings, and put off by the villagers' superstitions, Dr. Ellis decided to return to Mérida. Mrs. Vargas was relieved to see him go, but cried in spite of herself. The children walked along behind the Land Cruiser as he slowly made his way back through the village towards the main road.

As Dr. Ellis headed for the highway north, the villagers wondered if his visit would bring them bad luck; the priest wondered if God had taken care of the dead man's soul, although all of the prayers had been said in Dr. Ellis' name; and Mrs. Vargas decided that her sister in Mérida owed her a big favor.

In the jungle, under the tangle of vines and fallen trees, the rockbird stomped and shook out its golden feathers on its carefully groomed square yard of bare ground, little knowing that it was the cause of so much trouble.

The mystery of the dead American was never solved. The mayor received a letter from the American consulate, saying that a representative would be sent to investigate, but no one ever came. Two or three people claimed to have seen the old man standing outside of the village at dusk in his tattered raincoat. It was an evil spirit all along, said some, come to stir up trouble in the village. If the coffin were to be opened, nothing would be found inside but corn husks. But Mrs. Vargas never doubted the reality of the man she had helped prepare for burial.

The night that Mrs. Vargas awoke with moonlight on the foot of the bed and heard a noise outside, she knew that the dead man had returned. A wind blew from the east, whistling around the edges of the house. A lonely dog was barking. Mrs. Vargas got up and walked barefoot into the front room in her long, cotton nightgown, her black and silver braids down her back. She knew what she had to do. Feeling for the worn leather portfolio which had taken up residence under the sofa, Mrs. Vargas then unlatched the front door.

Even in the moonlight, his complexion looked unhealthy, his coat dusty and torn. The wind made wisps of hair stand up on his head, then lie down again.

Not daring to speak, Mrs. Vargas threw the portfolio as far as she could away from the house, across the road into the waiting jungle. The man bowed slightly, a wistful look on his face, and turned away. Mrs. Vargas slammed the door, locked it, and returned to her bedroom. And all the living, and all the dead, were in place.

QUESTIONS TO CONSIDER

1. What are the village's traditions on the occasion of a death?

2. What are some differences between the two men who visit Mrs. Vargas's house?

3. Why were villagers reluctant to trust the real Dr. Ellis?

Visions of Cuba I

BY JOSÉ MARTÍ AND PABLO MEDINA

Poet, journalist, and freedom fighter José Martí (1853–1895) was born in Cuba but later lived in Mexico and traveled through Central America, Santo Domingo, and Jamaica. Martí's struggle for Cuban independence forced him to exile in the United States, where he lived the last fourteen years of his brief life. He is the author of Versos sencillos, Ismaelillo, and La edad de oro. His Complete Works fill two dozen volumes. This excerpt from "Dos Patrias" is about nostalgia for his homeland, which he pictures as a sorrowful widow.

Poet and novelist Pablo Medina (1948–   ) is known for his insightful reflections on exile and displacement. His books include Exiled Memories, The Marks of Birth, Arching into the Afterlife, and The Return of Felix Nogara. The poem "Flight Out of Miami" is about longing.

Dos Patrias

by José Martí
translated by Ilan Stavans

Dos patrias tengo yo: Cuba y la noche.
¿O son una las dos? No bien retira
Su majestad el sol, con largos velos
Y un clavel en la mano, silenciosa
Cuba cual viuda triste me aparece.
¡Yo sé cuál es ese clavel sangriento
Que en la mano le tiembla! Está vacío
Mi pecho, destrozado está y vacío
En donde estaba el corazón.

I have two motherlands: Cuba and the night.
Or are they one and the same?
As soon as the sun withdraws
Its majesty, with long veils
And a carnation in her hand, silently
Cuba appears to me like a sad widow.
I know what that bloody carnation is
that trembles in her hand! Empty
my breast, destroyed and empty
Where once was my heart.

Flight Out of Miami

by Pablo Medina

I am going away.
I am leaving the heat,
the fierce sun,
the spread of concrete
over marshland.
I cannot stand still
and make this home.

Even your slim fingers
and your Cuban eyebrows
speak of displacement,
anguish in control.
I am lost in the fragrance
of gardenias, the palmetto[1]
shadow's dim replacement,
in your face like the city,
roads over water, water
over dreams,
the overwhelming strangeness
of the American landscape,
and your lips
straining to say
what you cannot remember.

---

[1] palmetto—small tropical plant with fan-shaped leaves.

QUESTIONS TO CONSIDER

1. With what traditional symbols does Martí dress
   the widow?

2. How do Martí and Medina use flowers as symbols in
   their poems?

3. What does Medina dislike about Miami?

4. Why does Medina say the "you" of the poem
   "cannot remember"?

Promised Lands

BY TINO VILLANUEVA

*Poet Tino Villanueva (1941–   ) was active in the Chicano Movement,
a Mexican-American civil rights movement of the 1960s and 1970s.
He currently teaches at Boston University. His books include the
bilingual collection,* Chronicle of My Worst Years *(Spanish, 1987;
translated in 1994 by James Hoggard), from which the following poem
about a family of migrant workers is excerpted. In 1994, his book*
Scenes from the Movie "Giant" *won the American Book Award.*

Many a morning
it was easy not to wake up,
but already discolored figures
were entering and leaving
through the half-dreamt house
carrying I don't know what kind of boxes
as if they were on a timetable.
How can I forget eating breakfast
without being aware of it,
or how suddenly metal rang
against metal

as a green two-wheeled trailer
was hooked up
to haul bundles
of household goods.

Now all the journeys
are one: very early
and hopeful, we left
by the empty
asphalt highway
(I always remember a black car),
we left secretly,
well before first light,
like people who wanted
to be spared the shame of living.
And I felt like not going, like resting
from earlier times.
Each summer we reappeared
because the land toward the south
(El Campo, Wharton, Taiton,
New Taiton, Glen Flora)
promised cotton bolls[1] and green fields;
because there was no way
to lighten that life's life,
to redeem us
from one single excessively sunny
afternoon when the body
was soaked with sweat,
and the sun's daggers
let us have it in the back.
(Please, who will come one day for me
to cure me of the horror
of being here, to quench
my thirst forever?)

---

[1] bolls—seed pods.

Far on into September,
the plants already dried up,
I continued being the **indolent**[2] child,
because I had no other hope
than for us to go
north up the road
(Hale Center, Plainview,
Levelland, Seymour, Seminole)
where suddenly we were already
choking with the cold sand,
where we were racing the clock again
elbow to elbow
like a **congenitally**[3] humpbacked mass
spread out through the state
                    wrapped up
stooped over   kneeling
through the brittle frost
and scratched by the scythelike stalks
as we gave the necessary pull and snap
to dry-hulled bolls.
We went through the month of January,
and a light wind bit us
each time we lifted our faces.
There also only the clods
were ours, not the land.
(I wished I were a jackrabbit so I could make
the great leap, to run,
to run away and not come back.)

---

[2] **indolent**—habitually lazy.

[3] **congenitally**—inherently; by way of birth.

Because of all
I'm concerned with today,
I give more thought now
to how prisonlike that childhood was
in the **abhorrent**[4] world
of cotton-field work.
Who gave the order in the '40s
the furrows had to be so long,
and the time
that dragged in picking them
should slaver[5] to devour me?
In the '50s the answer
was already unimportant to me. I told myself:
everything's lost, get up and go
as best you can. You're not getting anything here.
I couldn't separate past from future
till the '60s,
and leave the hot unshaded roads behind,
and the ones frozen over.

---

[4] **abhorrent**—hateful.
[5] slaver—slobber.

QUESTIONS TO CONSIDER

1. What images does the speaker use to evoke the feeling of working in someone else's fields?

2. How can the speaker's childhood be both indolent and prisonlike?

3. Based on this poem, what do you think a migrant family's life is like?

Tradition

Religion has played an important role in Latino communities all over the United States. In this church in Trampas, New Mexico, statues of saints are common property, so the many devout parishioners, such as these four men, may take them home for the night.

▲
A ceramic sculpture garden in this Mexican district of Texas shows one woman's devotion to her religion and culture.

Many Latinos view family togetherness as an essential part of everyday life. Children often live with their parents until they are married, and many choose to stay close to home even after they move away. This tightly knit family in Santa Fe has gathered to celebrate Christmas.

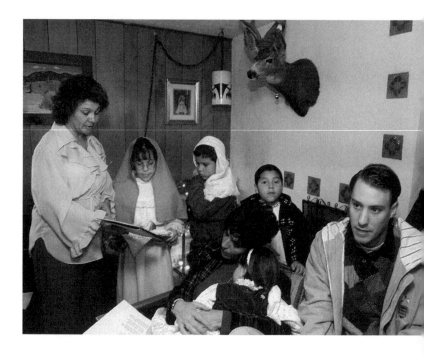

▲
One of Florida's most lively areas, Little Havana enjoys the country's highest population of Cuban Americans. Here recent Cuban immigrants and later generations of Cubans live, work, and celebrate their culture as though they were in Cuba itself. Cuban restaurants and street vendors abound in little Havana. This man offers freshly cooked spareribs among other Cuban delights from his stand.

▲

Cesar Chavez (center) joins a group of protestors at a farm workers' rally.
In the early 1960s Chavez succeeded in organizing the first agricultural workers'
union, the United Farm Workers.

Little Havana, the Cuban area of Miami, Florida, was a hotbed of political activity during the controversy surrounding six-year-old Cuban refugee Elián Gonzalez. The United States was split on whether to return Elián to his father in Cuba or let him stay with his extended family in Little Havana. Here, a crowd waves flags to demonstrate its support of the United States' decision to return the boy to Cuba.

Mexican culture thrives in many parts of the western United States. Above, folk dancers commemorate the opening of a plaza in East Los Angeles.

Dancers reenact the more ancient traditions of their Indian ancestors outside a church in the Tesuque Pueblo of New Mexico. ▶

Family

from

When I Was Puerto Rican

BY ESMERALDA SANTIAGO

Esmeralda Santiago (1948–   ) is a novelist and memoirist whose books include When I Was Puerto Rican, America's Dream, *and* Almost a Woman. *She is also the editor, along with Joie Davidow, of the popular anthologies* Las Christmas *and* Las Mamis. *Santiago, the oldest of eleven children, moved with her family from Puerto Rico to New York City in 1961, when she was thirteen years old.*

For months after the hurricane all people talked about was money. Money for the cement and cinder blocks that rose out of the ground in solid, grey walls and flat square roofs. Money for another cow, or a car, or zinc for the new outhouse. Money to install water pipes, or to repair the electric wires that had gone down in the storm and hung like limp, useless, dried-up worms.

Even children talked about money. We scoured the side of the road for discarded bottles to exchange for pennies when the glass man came around. Boys no older than I nailed together boxes out of wood scraps, painted them in bright colors, and set off for San Juan or Rio Piedras, where men paid ten cents for a shoeshine. Papi made *maví*, bark beer, and took two gallons with him to the construction sites where he worked, to sell by the cup to his friends and passersby. Even Doña Lola, who seemed as self-sufficient as anyone could be in [the town of] Macún, cooked huge vats of rice and beans to sell in the refillable aluminum canisters called *fiambreras* that men took to work when their jobs were not near places to eat. Mami talked about sewing school uniforms and actually made a few. But she soon realized that the amount of work she put into them was more than she was paid for and abandoned the idea while she thought of something else.

"Negi, help me over here."

Mami stood in the middle of the room, her dress bunched on her hips, hands holding fast a long-line brassiere that didn't want to contain her. "See if you can catch the hooks into the eyes, all the way up."

The cotton brassiere stretched down to her hipbones, where it met the girdle into which she had already squeezed. There were three columns of eyes for the hooks spaced evenly from top to bottom. Even when I tugged on both ends of the fabric, I had trouble getting one hook into an outermost eye.

"It's too small. I can't get them to meet."

"I'll hold my breath." She took in air, blew it out, and stretched her spine up. I worked fast, hooking her up all the way before she had to breathe again in big, hungry gulps.

"Wow! It's been a while since I wore this thing," she said, pulling her dress up. "Zip me up?"

"Where are you going?"

"There's a new factory opening in [the town of] Toa Baja. Maybe they need people who can sew."

"Who's going to take care of us?"

"Gloria will be here in a little while. You can help her with the kids. I've already made dinner."

"Will you work every day?"

"If they hire me."

"So you won't be around all the time."

"We need the money, Negi."

Mami twisted and sprayed her hair, powdered her face, patted rouge on already pink cheeks, and spread lipstick over already red lips. Her feet, which were usually bare, looked unnatural in high heels. Her waist was so pinched in, it seemed as if part of her body were missing. Her powdered and painted features were not readable; the lines she'd drawn on her eyebrows and around her eyes and the colors that enhanced what always seemed perfect were a violation of the face that sometimes laughed and sometimes cried and often **contorted**[1] with rage. I wanted to find a rag and wipe that stuff off her face, the way she wiped off the dirt and grime that collected on mine. She turned to me with a large red smile.

"What do you think?"

I was ashamed to look, afraid to speak what I saw.

"Well?" She put her hands on her hips, that familiar gesture of exasperation that always made her seem larger, and I saw the unnatural diamond shape formed by her elbows and narrowed waist. I couldn't help the tears that broke my face into a million bits, which made her kneel and hold me. I wrapped my arms around her, but what I felt was not Mami but the harsh bones of her undergarments. I buried my face in the soft space between her neck and shoulder and sought there the fragrance of oregano and rosemary, but all I could come up with was

---

[1] **contorted**—twisted.

Cashmere Bouquet and the faint flowery dust of Maybelline. . . .[2]

Mami was one of the first mothers in Macún to have a job outside the house. For extra money women in the *barrio*[3] took in laundry or ironing or cooked for men with no wives. But Mami left our house every morning, primped and perfumed, for a job in a factory in Toa Baja.

The *barrio* looked at us with new eyes. Gone was the bland acceptance of people minding their own business, replaced by a visible, angry resentment that became gossip, and **taunts**[4] and name-calling in the school yard.

I got the message that my mother was breaking a taboo[5] I'd never heard about. The women in the neighborhood turned their backs on her when they saw her coming, or, when they talked to her, they scanned the horizon, as if looking at her would infect them with whatever had made her go out and get a job. Only a few of the neighbors stood by Mami—Doña Ana, whose daughter watched us, Doña Zena, whose Christian beliefs didn't allow for envy, and Doña Lola, who valued everyone equally. Even Tío Candido's wife, Meri, made us feel as if Mami was a bad woman for leaving us alone.

I was confused by the effect my mother's absence caused in other people.

"Why, Mami? Why is everyone so mean just because you have a job?" I pleaded one day after a schoolmate said Mami was not getting her money from a factory but from men in the city.

"They're jealous," she said. "They can't imagine a better life for themselves, and they're not willing to let anyone else have it either. Just ignore them."

---

[2] oregano . . . Maybelline—Oregano and rosemary are fragrant plants used in cooking. Cashmere Bouquet is a soap, and Maybelline is a brand of make-up.

[3] *barrio*—Spanish-speaking neighborhood.

[4] **taunts**—jeers.

[5] taboo—societal ban.

But I couldn't close my ears to their insults, couldn't **avert**[6] my eyes quickly enough to miss their hate-filled looks. I was abandoned by children who until then had been friends. The neighbors on the long walk to and from home were no longer friendly; they no longer offered me a drink of water on a hot afternoon or a dry porch when it rained.

Papi seemed to have the same opinion about Mami's job as the neighbors. He looked at her with a puzzled expression, and several times I heard her defend herself: "If it weren't for the money I bring in, we'd still be living like savages." He'd withdraw to his hammers and nails, to the mysterious books in his dresser, to the newspapers and magazines he brought home rolled up in his wooden toolbox.

I had worried that not having Mami around would make our lives harder, but at first it made things easier. Mami was happy with her work, proud of what she did, eager to share with us the adventures of her day in the factory, where she stitched cotton brassieres she said had to be for American women because they were too small to fit anyone we knew.

But her days were long, filled in the morning with the chores of making both breakfast and dinner, getting seven children ready for school or a day with Gloria, preparing for work, going there and back, returning to a basketful of mending, a house that needed sweeping, a floor that needed mopping, sheets that had to be washed and dried in one day because we didn't have two sets for each bed. As she settled into her routine, Mami decided she needed help, and she turned to me.

"You are the oldest, and I expect you to be responsible for your sisters and brothers, and to do more around the house."

---

[6] **avert**—turn away.

"But isn't Gloria going to take care of us?"

"I can't count on anyone from outside the family. Besides, you're old enough to be more responsible."

And with those words Mami sealed a pact she had designed, written, and signed for me.

"Delsa, you'd better get in here and do the dishes before Mami gets home."

Delsa looked up from the numbers she wrote in her composition book. Rows and rows of numbers, over and over again, in neat columns, in her small, tight script. "It's not my turn." She went back to her homework.

"Whose turn is it then?"

"Yours. I did it yesterday."

The sink was full. Plates, cups, spoons, pot lids, the heavy aluminum rice pot, the frying pan, all half submerged in gray water with a greasy scum floating on the top. "Norma!"

"What!"

"Come here. I'm going to teach you to wash dishes."

"I'm watching Raymond."

"Well, let Hector watch him."

"I don't want to."

"If these dishes aren't washed by the time Mami comes home . . . "

"You do them, then."

I didn't want to either. I didn't want to do any of the things Mami asked of me: feed the kids an after-school snack; make sure they did their homework; get Raymond and Edna from Gloria's; change the water on the beans and put them on the stove to cook over low heat; sweep the floor; make the beds; mound the dirty clothes in the basket; feed the chickens and the pigs. Delsa and Norma were supposed to help, but most of the time they refused, especially when I tried to get them to do the unpleasant tasks like changing Raymond's diaper or scrubbing the rice pot. Almost every day just before Mami came home I scrambled around to do all the things she'd asked me to take care of that morning. And almost every day I received either a lecture or *cocotazos*[7] for not doing everything.

"You're almost *señorita*. You should know to do this without being told."

"I just can't . . . "

"You're lazy, that's your problem. You think everything will be handed to you."

"No I don't," I whimpered, my hands protecting my head from the inevitable blows.

"Don't you talk back!" And she pushed me away as if I were contagious. "The least you can do is set an example for your sisters and brothers."

I looked at Delsa, who at nine could already make perfect rice, and at Norma, who swept and mopped with precision, and at Hector, who dutifully changed out of his uniform into play clothes every day without being told. "What makes them so good and me so bad?" I asked myself. But there were no answers in Delsa's solemn eyes, or in Norma's haughty beauty, or in Hector's eagerness to please. Every night Mami told me how I had failed in my duty as a female, as a sister, as the eldest. And every day I proved her right by neglecting my chores, by letting one of the kids get hurt, by burning the beans, by not commanding the respect from my sisters and brothers that I was owed as the oldest.

---

[7] *cocotazos*—blows on the head.

QUESTIONS TO CONSIDER

1. Why does Mami get a job?

2. How does Mami's job affect family life?

3. Why is the speaker unable to satisfy her mother?

Birthday

BY DAGOBERTO GILB

Dagoberto Gilb was born into a Mexican-American family in 1954 and now lives in El Paso, Texas. He is the author of The Magic of Blood, *which won the 1994 Ernest Hemingway Foundation Award, and* The Last Known Residence of Mickey Acuña, *named a Notable Book of the Year by the* New York Times Book Review. *The following story, first published in 1987, is told from the point of view of a man remembering when he was six years old. Notice how Gilb uses sentence structure and language to create this young voice.*

There was traffic on his birthday. The Hollywood Freeway to the downtown area. His father sighed and got off and got back on going in the other direction and then jumped on again saying he'd catch the 5 Freeway and then they got there but the ramp was closed for repair. His father started grumbling and talking about how he should have thought of this before, that he shouldn't have promised to go to that toy store because it was so far away and saying he couldn't understand how people could live like this all the time, back home nothing was as complicated as here, when he was a kid he didn't have toys like they have now and kids didn't expect as much. His mother said that maybe they should go somewhere else, to the shopping center, that toy store will be open and he can pick out what he wants over there, that'll be all right. His father said he should have called around like a smart man, that he didn't even know really if the store way out here had the toy the boy wanted. The boy, who was six today, let his happy pucker loosen from his lips and his body sag into the backseat as they drove in what seemed to him like a direction of home. But then his father, eyes at him in the rearview mirror, said no. I told him we'd go there, he expects to go and I'm going to take him there and I think I even have an idea. And he drove a little faster, made a turn and another, and got on the Glendale Freeway and then onto the 5 and boomed okay! and we're gonna get there now and it's my son's birthday and it is his day.

It was a long drive and the boy, his arms looped over the front seat now between his parents, worried that this wasn't right either. Was his daddy sure? Was he sure they shouldn't turn around or maybe they weren't going the right way, or maybe they'd gone too far, he'd never seen this freeway before and it didn't look like the one the toy store was next to last time. His mother said look over there, it must be a zoo she teased, because there's a picture of a giraffe on the building. It was the toy store and his baby brother was excited too and pointed ah ah! but his baby sister still slept. The boy controlled his body but not his smile and said oh yeah mommy that must be the zoo so let's go to the zoo and everybody laughed and felt happy and good and they parked and set up a collapsible stroller, the freeway visible and roaring beside them, and, pushing the thick glass doors, they went inside.

It was at least twelve feet high with toys, a trucker's warehouse big, more toys than all the days of childhood, all squeals and squeaks and putts, little kids running and whining and wanting, bouncing and rolling things. The father and the mother and the two boys and the baby sister each were twisting their necks and stopping, look at this, look at this. Get anything you want, the father told his six-year-old, but he didn't say but not for too much, he couldn't talk about money on his son's birthday, didn't want to explain about paying bills, all the other expenses, problems, how it was in this new place. There's so many things, the boy said, it's so hard. Well, get what you want, what we came here for, that one you saw last time. I just don't know if it's the best one, the boy said, and his father said oh yes it is, it's the best one in the whole place, and his father thought that the price was right too, and he said it's got 145 pieces and a big mountain, and tanks, and landing craft to cross the river, and fighter planes. The boy wanted to know who the good guys were and who were the bad guys and how could you tell? His father said he guessed it was those Germans, yeah these are the Nazi men and they were bad men, they really were bad guys and the Americans really were good guys. And the boy smiled and his father found a new unopened box almost as tall as the boy who glowed with excitement. They were all ready to go home now but the mother wanted to buy some party plates and the younger boy had to get something so he didn't cry so they chose an $.87 package of horses and for the baby girl a soft, pink bracelet-like teething ring for $1.19. They stood in line to pay. There were long lines. The boy waited contentedly, but the other two could not and the mother took them away. The boy just stared at his box, at the pictures, and his father stood there and waited with all the other waiting people. When he got to the stand he asked the young girl is it always crowded like this? and she said always and he shook his head. Life in the big city, she said, and he said life in the big city, and he paid, and the boy pulled the box off the counter, I want to carry it myself, and everyone in the family seemed as happy as him.

The boy had picked out a cake at the supermarket the night before. He didn't want his mother to make it, he knew exactly where the cakes that he wanted were and he guided them through the aisles of the market and squinted at the plastic windows of the cake boxes. His mother and father suggested one but he said no, not that, and found one with a clown and said this one. His father and mother saw the price and said that's a little too expensive and inside it's pink strawberry but the boy had already changed his mind, saying this is it, this one, this one here. It was chocolate devil's food with three white flowers and green leaves and white spiraled frosting in longhand[1] happy birthday. How about this other one? his mother asked. It's the same, except I can write happy birthday on it, and it's less expensive. No, the boy said, this is the one, please, this is the one. Well if you get that, his mother told him, we probably can't get ice cream. His father's silence agreed, and the boy thought about it, then said okay and picked up the chocolate cake anyway. I'll get it, his father said, and he carried it but said we have to get ice cream and the mother helped choose the brand of vanilla.

His mother stabbed six candles into the brown frosting. She arranged them so there were five blue ones at each corner of an imaginary star and one yellow one in the middle. His father posed the boy next to the cake and took a picture, then he found some matches and lit the candles, and then his mother and father sang, only their voices, the father's loud, the mother's soft, the baby girl in her arms drooling, the younger boy, eyes open, learning. It was overcast outside the window near this. The man next door who nagged and screamed at his wife was sweet-talking his dog, and there was a

---

[1] longhand—cursive writing.

police helicopter swirling around and black-and-whites[2] filling up the street behind them. A radio not so far away played a love song by Yolanda del Río. The father snapped a picture with a flash of the boy blowing out the candles. His mother brought out two more presents, each wrapped in paper that had been around the house, without ribbon or bows. She said, the little one's from your brother and sister, the big one's from your mommy and daddy. The little one was comic books and the boy smiled, so pleased, and grabbed the other and ripped it open. It was called the Sword of Grayskull, which was from his favorite TV show, and now he was happy beyond words. His mother cut up the cake and his father scooped out ice cream and they all sat around quietly eating off the party plates. The radio outside was off and instead they heard a police bullhorn mumbling on the street behind them. His father told the boy to wait a minute, he thought he had a couple of batteries. He loaded them in the black plastic handle of the sword and then handed it to the boy. The six-year-old held it above his head with both hands and lit up the yellow plastic blade. Slicing the darkening air, his whole family admired him as he stood in the center of the room saying I have the power!

---

[2] black-and-whites—police cars.

QUESTIONS TO CONSIDER

1. What worries the boy on the way to the toy store?

2. How do the mother and father cooperate with the boy to make the birthday special?

3. Why do you think Gilb mentions the police helicopter, police cars, and police bullhorn?

Eva and Daniel

BY TOMÁS RIVERA

*Tomás Rivera (1935–1984) is one of the major figures in Chicano
literature. He was born in Crystal City, Texas, the son of migrant
workers. An educator, Rivera taught high school and university
courses in Spanish literature and eventually became Chancellor of
the University of California, Riverside. His novel . . .* And the Earth
Did Not Devour Him *is a classic. His* Complete Works, *from
which this tale of young love is taken, was published in 1992.*

People still remember Eva and Daniel. They were
both very good looking, and in all honesty it was a
pleasure to see them together. But that's not the reason
people remember them. They were very young when
they got married or, rather, when they **eloped**.[1] Her
parents hardly got angry at all, and, if they did, it was for
a very short time and that was because everyone who
knew Daniel liked him very much and had many good
reasons to like him. They eloped up north during the
County Fair that was held every year in Bird Island.

---

[1] **eloped**—ran away together.

Both families lived on the same ranch. They worked together in the same fields, they went to town in the same truck and they just about had their meals together; they were that close. That's why no one was surprised when they started going together. And, even though everyone knew about it, no one let on, and even Eva and Daniel, instead of talking with one another, would write letters to each other once in a while. I remember very clearly that that Saturday when they eloped they were going happily to the fair in the truck. Their hair was all messed up by the wind, but when they got to the fair they didn't even remember to comb it.

They got on every ride, then they separated from the group and no one saw them again until two days later.

* * *

"Don't be afraid. We can take a taxi to the ranch. Move over this way, come closer, let me touch you. Don't you love me?"

"Yes, yes."

"Don't be afraid. We'll get married. I don't care about anything else. Just you. If the truck leaves us behind, we'll go back in a taxi."

"But they're going to get after me."

"Don't worry. If they do, I'll protect you myself. Anyway, I want to marry you. I'll ask your father for permission to court you if you want me to. What do you say? Shall we get married?"

* * *

At midnight, when all the games were closed and the lights of the fair were turned off and the explosions of the fireworks were no longer heard, Eva and Daniel still hadn't shown up. Their parents started to worry then, but they didn't notify the police. By one-thirty in the morning the other people became impatient. They got on and off the truck every few minutes and, finally, Eva's father told the driver to drive off. Both families were worried. They had a feeling that Eva and Daniel had eloped and they were sure they would get married, but they were worried anyway. And they would keep on worrying until they saw them again. What they didn't know was that Eva and Daniel were already at the ranch. They were hiding in the barn, up in the loft where the boss stored hay for the winter. That's why, even though they looked for them in the nearby towns, they didn't find them until two days later when they came down from the loft very hungry.

There were some very heated discussions but, finally, Eva's parents consented to their marriage. The following day they took Eva and Daniel to get their blood test, then a week later they took them before the judge and the parents had to sign because they were too young.

* * *

"You see how everything turned out all right."

"Yes, but I was afraid when father got all angry. I even thought he was going to hit you when he saw us for the first time."

"I was afraid too. We're married now. We can have children."

"Yes."

"I hope that they grow real tall and that they look like you and me. I wonder how they will be?"

"Just let them be like you and me."

"If it's a girl I hope she looks like you; if it's a boy I hope he looks like me."

"What if we don't have any?"

"Why not? My family and your family are very large."

"I'll say."

"Well, then?"

"I was just talking."

Things really began to change after they were married. First of all because, by the end of the first month of their marriage, Eva was vomiting often, and then also Daniel received a letter from the government telling him to be in such and such town so that he could take his physical for the army.[2] He was afraid when he saw the letter, not so much for himself, but he immediately sensed the separation that would come forever.

"You see, son, if you hadn't gone to school you wouldn't have passed the examination."

"Oh, mama. They don't take you just because you passed the examination. Anyway I'm already married, so they probably won't take me. And another thing, Eva is already expecting."

"I don't know what to do, son, every night I pray that they won't take you. So does Eva. You should have lied to them. You should have played dumb so you wouldn't pass."

"Oh, come on, mama."

*   *   *

By November, instead of returning to Texas with his family, Daniel stayed up north, and in a few days he was in the army. The days didn't seem to have any meaning for him—why should there be night, morning or day. Sometimes he didn't care anything about anything. Many times he thought about escaping and returning to his own town so that he could be with Eva. When he thought at all, that was what he thought about—Eva. I

---

[2] This story takes place during the Korean War (1950–1953), when young men were drafted into the armed services.

think he even became sick, once or maybe it was several times, thinking so much about her. The first letter from the government had meant their separation, and now the separation became longer and longer.

*   *   *

"I wonder why I can't think of anything else other than Eva? If I hadn't known her, I wonder what I would think about. Probably about myself, but now . . . "

*   *   *

Things being what they were, everything marched on. Daniel's training continued at the same pace as Eva's pregnancy. They transferred Daniel to California, but before going he had the chance to be with Eva in Texas. The first night they went to sleep kissing. They were happy once again for a couple of weeks but then right away they were separated again. Daniel wanted to stay but then he decided to go on to California. He was being trained to go to Korea. Later Eva started getting sick. The baby was bringing complications. The closer she came to the day of delivery, the greater the complications.

*   *   *

"You know, viejo,[3] something is wrong with that baby."
"Why do you say that?"
"Something is wrong with her. She gets very high fevers at night. I hope everything turns out all right, but even the doctor looks quite worried. Have you noticed?"
"No."
"Yesterday he told me that we had to be very careful with Eva. He gave us a whole bunch of instructions, but it's difficult when you can't understand him. Can you

---

[3] viejo—dear (used with a parent or a spouse).

imagine? How I wish Daniel were here. I'll bet you Eva would even get well. I already wrote to him saying that she is very sick, hoping that he'll come to see her, but maybe his superiors won't believe him and won't let him come."

"Well, write to him again. Maybe he can arrange something, if he speaks out."

"Maybe, but I've already written him a number of letters saying the same thing. You know, I'm not too worried about him anymore. Now I worry about Eva. They're both so young."

"Yes they are, aren't they."

*   *   *

Eva's condition became worse and, when he received a letter from his mother in which she begged him to come see his wife, either Daniel didn't make himself understood or his superiors didn't believe him. They didn't let him go. He went AWOL[4] just before he was to be sent to Korea. It took him three days to get to Texas on the bus. But he was too late.

I remember very well that he came home in a taxi. When he got down and heard the cries coming from inside the house he rushed in. He went into a rage and threw everyone out of the house and locked himself in for almost the rest of the day. He only went out when he had to go to the toilet, but even in there he could be heard sobbing.

He didn't go back to the army and no one ever bothered to come looking for him. Many times I saw him burst into tears. I think he was remembering. Then he lost all interest in himself. He hardly spoke to anyone.

One time he decided to buy fireworks to sell during Christmas time. The package of fireworks which he sent for through a magazine advertisement cost him plenty. When he got them, instead of selling them, he didn't

---

[4] AWOL—absent without leave.

stop until he had set them all off himself. Since that time that's all he does with what little money he earns to support himself. He sets off fireworks just about every night. I think that's why around this part of the country people still remember Eva and Daniel. Maybe that's it.

QUESTIONS TO CONSIDER

1. Why does everyone in their families go along with the marriage of Eva and Daniel?

2. What do you think Daniel and Eva could have done differently so their lives would have been better?

from

The Hispanic Condition

BY ILAN STAVANS

Ilan Stavans (1961–   ) is a professor at Amherst College and a renowned cultural critic. He was born in Mexico and is well known for his interpretations of Latino culture. His books include Art and Anger, The Riddle of Cantinflas, *and his memoir* On Borrowed Words. *His best work is anthologized in* The Essential Ilan Stavans. The Hispanic Condition *(1995) is a collective memoir of the Hispanic people north of the Rio Grande, that is, in the United States. In the following excerpt, from the introduction, Stavans writes that the book is essentially a story of family.*

Letter to My Child
Adorado Mío:

I once had a dream in which I was given a copy of an unknown work of cultural analysis,[1] *Caliban's*[2]

---

[1] cultural analysis—examination and critique of a particular culture or society.

[2] *Caliban's*—belonging to a wild character from Shakespeare's play *The Tempest* who lives alone on an island until a shipwrecked man enslaves him. See also page 130.

Utopia:[3] or, *Barbarism*[4] *Reconsidered.* When I woke up, it was next to me. I carefully opened it and, quite shocked, realized its pages were totally blank. A moment later, the volume was magically gone—vanished through the invisible rabbets[5] of reality. I never found it again. I have tried in vain to summon its content, most of which, I have come to believe, dealt with *América*—the word, the idea, the reality. Look for it! At some point in your promisingly young life, you may be the lucky one to put your fingers on it. Meanwhile, I would like to talk to you today about exile, language, democracy, and what it means for me to be a citizen of the United States, my adopted country.

* * *

I come from an intellectually sophisticated, financially unstable middle-class family in Mexico's capital, a secure, self-imposed Jewish **ghetto**,[6] an autistic[7] island where **gentiles**[8] hardly existed and Hebraic symbols prevailed. Money and comfort, books, theater, and art. What made me Mexican? It's hard to know: language and the air I breathed, perhaps. Early on I was sent to Yiddish[9] day school, Colegio Israelita de México in Colonia Narvarte, where the heroes were S. Y. Agnon, Sholem Aleichem, and Theodor Herzl,[10] while people like Lázaro Cárdenas, José Joaqun Fernández de Lizardi, and Alfonso Reyes[11] were our neighbors' models, not ours. Surrounded by the Other, I, together

---

[3] *Utopia*—ideal society.

[4] *Barbarism*—brutality.

[5] rabbets—grooves along the edge of a piece of wood.

[6] **ghetto**—minority area of a city.

[7] autistic—abnormally introverted.

[8] **gentiles**—non-Jews.

[9] Yiddish—like the language spoken by Jews of central European origin.

[10] Agnon, Aleichem, Herzl—Jewish authors and historical figures.

[11] Cárdenas, Fernández de Lizardi, Reyes—Mexican statesmen and writers.

with my family and friends, inhabited a self-sufficient island, with imaginary borders built in agreement between us and the outside world, an **oasis**,[12] completely uninvolved with things Mexican. In fact, when it came to knowledge of the outside world, Jewish students like me, and probably the whole middle class, were far better off talking about U.S. products (Hollywood, syndicated[13] shows like "Star Trek," junk food, and technology) than about Mexico—an artificial capsule, our habitat. The neighboring country across the border was for me and my schoolmates the perfect image of "paradise on earth." Money permitting, as a child and adolescent I would accompany my family on vacation trips to Texas, Florida, and California, in shopping sprees to acquire, to be part of a type of postindustrial modernity[14] personified by the hard-to-understand English-speaking Anglo consumers in Houston's mall La Galería and by Disneyland, a **microcosm**[15] where synthetic birds sing in the Tikki Tikki Room, where you take a tour through the human anatomy that begins in a microscope, eat hot dogs next to Mickey Mouse, and where, on a fake stage, the pirate Sir Francis Drake, on his ship *Golden Hind*, **pillages**[16] the coasts of South America in front of your very eyes. Expansive, **imperialistic**,[17] a never-ending parade of naive monolingual[18] tourists with cameras in hand to seize the memory, the have-a-good-times of narrow-mindedness, I perceived Americans to be money driven, ready to sell Taco Bell in the land of tacos and never stop at anything to make a deal. Aside from the **ubiquitous**[19]

---

[12] **oasis**—refuge.

[13] syndicated—sold to local television stations.

[14] postindustrial modernity—life after the Industrial Revolution.

[15] **microcosm**—little model of reality.

[16] **pillages**—loots.

[17] **imperialistic**—extending authority over lands other than one's own.

[18] monolingual—able to speak only one language.

[19] **ubiquitous**—widespread.

hamburger, a German import, the national cuisine, I thought, was just a sum of international palates: burritos and chili con carne, pizza and spaghetti, Caesar salad, onion soup, and crepes. Whereas the United States, where the future has already happened and history is a recent invention, was Paradise-on-Wheels, Mexico was stuck in the past, which acquires cyclic dimensions of trauma and discontent,[20] a past incredibly heavy and intrusive, a people unable to become, in a by-then already famous sentence, "contemporary with the rest of humankind."[21]

Everything changed at the age of twenty-five, when, as a foreign scholarship student, a counterpoint to Richard Rodríguez's vilified "scholarship boy,"[22] I was happily invited to the banquet in El Dorado and became part of the American scene. Farewell parties celebrated my early triumph. I was expected to take advantage of the exemplary academic resources across the border and become a writer and scholar. But after a few months, once I got a view from within, a deep transformation took place. Suddenly, I ceased to be Mexican and became, much to my surprise, a Latino— what's worse, a white Latino, something most people have difficulty understanding: Is every Peruvian brown skinned, every Nicaraguan short with black hair? Being from Aztecalandia,[23] I was automatically expected to have an Emiliano Zapata mustache;[24] carry a sombrero;[25] hide a tequila bottle; have an accent just

---

[20] cyclic dimensions of trauma and discontent—regularly repeating cycle of great upset and dissatisfaction.

[21] "contemporary with the rest of humankind"—modern.

[22] Richard Rodríguez's vilified "scholarship boy"—Mexican-American author's portrayal of an abused poor child.

[23] Aztecalandia—Mexico; literally, "land of the Aztecs."

[24] Emiliano Zapata mustache—thick mustache worn by a Mexican revolutionary hero.

[25] sombrero—hat with a wide brim worn in the southwestern United States and Mexico.

like Ricky Ricardo's,[26] making no distinction between long and short vowels ("live" and "leave"); and to take a siesta every afternoon from one to three-thirty. In short, I was yet another participant in the larger-than-life mirror of stereotypes.

I don't think I knew the meaning of the words *race* and *ethnicity* until I moved north. You see, Mexico is a multiracial society, in which Indians, Europeans, Asians, and Africans coexist more or less peacefully. But people refuse to acknowledge the mestizo heterogeneity.[27] On the contrary, the standard perception is that we all are particles of an altogether different transatlantic race. Furthermore, I was born Mexican without really knowing what that meant, and I did not learn what it meant until I came to the United States, where people automatically began addressing me as Hispanic. *Comprende español,* eh? people would ask. *Un poquito.*[28] Funny, you don't look Hispanic! Ever tried seafood burritos? And how do people say [*expletive*] in Mexican?

As you will one day find out, my dear, America, her triumphs and defeats, isn't only a nation (in [James] Baldwin's own words, "a state of mind") but also a vast continent. From Alaska to the Argentine pampas,[29] from Rio de Janeiro to East Los Angeles and Little Havana, the geography that the disoriented Genoese admiral Christopher Columbus mistakenly encountered in 1492 and Amerigo Vespucci[30] baptized a few years later is also a linguistic and cultural multiplicity,

---

[26] Ricky Ricardo's—belonging to a Cuban television character.

[27] mestizo heterogeneity—diversity of mixed-race peoples.

[28] *Un poquito*—A little.

[29] pampas—prairie.

[30] Amerigo Vespucci—Italian explorer after whom America was named.

a sum of parts: America the nation and America the continent. Thus, we the "Spanish-origin" people in the United States are truly twice American: as children of Thomas Jefferson and John Adams,[31] but, also, as citizens of the so-called New World. While some persist in seeing us as the newest wave of foreigners, second-class citizens at the bottom of the social hierarchy, at least three-fifths of us were in these territories even before the Pilgrims arrived on the *Mayflower,* and only unexpectedly, unwillingly became part of the United States when the Treaty of Guadalupe Hidalgo was signed. Twice American, once in spite of ourselves: American *americanos.*

In the book that accompanies this letter, I have done my best to map the **labyrinthine**[32] ways of my own journey and that of the Hispanic people north of the Rio Grande. Mine is a personal interpretation, partial and subjective. It needs to be added to a million others found daily on any street and classroom. I suspect that the sum of them all, my son, make the content of *Caliban's Utopia.* Find the volume. Be on the alert, looking for it wherever you go. When approached with wisdom, its virginal pages will explain Baldwin's odyssey and mine. Read its invisible paragraphs, then stamp your own divided words in indelible ink.

Todo mi amor, hoy y siempre.[33]

---

[31] Thomas Jefferson and John Adams—founders of the United States and early U.S. presidents.

[32] **labyrinthine**—twisting; like the confusing passageways of a labyrinth, or maze.

[33] *Todo mi amor, hoy y siempre*—All my love, today and forever.

QUESTIONS TO CONSIDER

1. What does the author want his son to know about his family history?

2. Based on the material in this letter, what do you think might be contained in the book *Caliban's Utopia: or, Barbarism Reconsidered*?

3. In what ways can life in America be considered "a state of mind"?

from

Dreaming in Cuban

BY CRISTINA GARCÍA

Cristina García was born in 1958 in Havana, Cuba, grew up in New York City, attended Barnard College, and worked for Time *magazine before becoming a novelist. A theme that occurs over and over in her writing is coming of age within a Latino family. Her books are* The Agüero Sisters *and* Dreaming in Cuban, *which was nominated for a National Book Award in 1992. This excerpt is addressed to García's daughter, Pilar.*

Pilar

My mother told me that Abuela[1] Celia was an **atheist**[2] before I even understood what the word meant. I liked the sound of it, the derision with which my mother pronounced it, and knew immediately it was what I wanted to become. I don't know exactly when I stopped believing in God. It wasn't as deliberate as

---

[1] Abuela—Grandmother.

[2] **atheist**—one who does not believe in any god.

deciding, at age six, to become an atheist, but more like an imperceptible **sloughing**[3] of layers. One day I noticed there was no more skin to absently peel, just air where there'd been **artifice**.[4]

A few weeks ago, I found photographs of Abuela Celia in my mother's hosiery drawer. There was a picture of Abuela in 1931, standing under a tree in her T-strap shoes and wearing a flouncy dress with a polka-dotted bow and puffed sleeves. Abuela Celia's fingers were tapered and delicate and rested on her hips. Her hair was parted on the right and came down to her shoulders, accentuating the mole by her lips. There was a tension at the corners of her mouth that could have **veered**[5] toward sadness or joy. Her eyes told of experience she did not yet possess.

There were other photographs. Abuela Celia in Soroa with an orchid in her hair. In a cream linen suit descending from a train. At the beach with my mother and my aunt. Tía Felicia is in Abuela's arms, a plump, pink-lozenge baby. My mother, unsmiling, skinny and dark from the sun, stands a distance away.

I have a trick to tell someone's public face from their private one. If the person is left-handed, like Abuela Celia, the right side of her face betrays her true feelings. I placed a finger over the left side of my grandmother's face, and in photograph after photograph I saw the truth.

*　*　*

I feel much more connected to Abuela Celia than to Mom, even though I haven't seen my grandmother in seventeen years. We don't speak at night anymore, but she's left me her legacy nonetheless—a love for the sea and the smoothness of pearls, an appreciation of music

---

[3] **sloughing**—shedding.

[4] **artifice**—clever deception.

[5] **veered**—turned.

and words, sympathy for the underdog, and a disregard for boundaries. Even in silence, she gives me the confidence to do what I believe is right, to trust my own perceptions.

This is a constant struggle around my mother, who systematically rewrites history to suit her views of the world. This reshaping of events happens in a dozen ways every day, contesting reality. It's not a matter of **premeditated**[6] deception. Mom truly believes that her version of events is correct, down to details that I know, for a fact, are wrong. To this day, my mother insists that I ran away from her at the Miami airport after we first left Cuba. But it was *she* who turned and ran when she thought she heard my father's voice. I wandered around lost until a pilot took me to his airline's office and gave me a lollipop.

It's not just our personal history that gets **mangled**.[7] Mom filters other people's lives through her distorting lens. Maybe it's that wandering eye of hers. It makes her see only what she wants to see instead of what's really there. Like Mr. Paresi, a pimpy[8] Brooklyn lawyer who my mother claims is the number-one criminal defense attorney in New York, complete with an impressive **roster**[9] of Mafia clients. And this because he comes to her shop every morning and buys two chocolate-frosted donuts for his breakfast.

Mom's **embellishments**[10] and half-truths usually equip her to tell a good story, though. And her English, her immigrant English, has a touch of otherness that makes it unintentionally precise. Maybe in the end the facts are not as important as the underlying truth she

---

[6] **premeditated**—planned.

[7] **mangled**—mutilated; ruined.

[8] pimpy—like a man who finds customers for prostitutes.

[9] **roster**—list.

[10] **embellishments**—fictitious details.

wants to convey. Telling her own truth is *the* truth to her, even if it's at the expense of chipping away our past.

I suppose I'm guilty in my own way of a creative transformation or two. Like my painting of the Statue of Liberty that caused such a commotion at the Yankee Doodle Bakery.[11] It's funny but last year the Sex Pistols ended up doing the same thing with a photograph of Queen Elizabeth on the cover of their *God Save the Queen* single. They put a safety pin through the Queen's nose and the entire country was up in arms. Anarchy in the U.K.,[12] I love it.

Mom is **fomenting**[13] her own brand of **anarchy**[14] closer to home. Her Yankee Doodle bakeries have become gathering places for these shady Cuban extremists who come all the way from New Jersey and the Bronx to talk their dinosaur politics and drink her killer espressos.[15] Last month they started a cablegram campaign against El Líder.[16] They set up a toll-free hot line so that Cuban exiles could call in and choose from three scathing messages to send directly to the National Palace, demanding El Líder's resignation.

I heard one of my mother's **cohorts**[17] boasting how last year he'd called in a bomb threat to the Metropolitan Opera House, where Alicia Alonso, the prima ballerina of the National Ballet of Cuba and a supporter of El Líder, was scheduled to dance. "I delayed *Giselle* for seventy-five minutes!" he bragged. If I'd known about it then, I would have sicked the FBI on him.

---

[11] Yankee Doodle Bakery—one of a chain of stores run by the author's mother.

[12] U.K.—United Kingdom (England, Scotland, Wales, and Northern Ireland).

[13] **fomenting**—promoting the growth of.

[14] **anarchy**—lawlessness and disorder.

[15] espressos—drinks of strong coffee.

[16] El Líder—Fidel Castro, Cuban revolutionary leader and president of Cuba.

[17] **cohorts**—associates.

Just last week, the lot of them were celebrating—with cigars and sparkling cider—the murder of a journalist in Miami who advocated reestablishing ties with Cuba. Those creeps passed around the Spanish newspaper and clapped each other on the back, as if they themselves had struck a big blow against the forces of evil. The front-page photograph showed the reporter's arm dangling from a poinciana tree on Key Biscayne after the bomb in his car had exploded.

I wonder how Mom could be Abuela Celia's daughter. And what I'm doing as my mother's daughter. Something got horribly scrambled along the way.

QUESTIONS TO CONSIDER

1. Why does the speaker prefer her abuela to her mother?

2. The speaker says that her mother did not practice "premeditated deception." What evidence does the speaker give to support this assertion?

3. How could the speaker learn to appreciate her mother more?

Mi Familia

BY CARMEN TAFOLLA

Carmen Tafolla (1951–   ) grew up in San Antonio, Texas, surrounded by a large family in a Mexican-American neighborhood. She has published children's books, such as Baby Coyote and the Old Woman, *as well as books for adults. This portion of "Autobiographical Notes" is from her book* Sonnets to Human Beings and Other Selected Works *(1995). In addition to being a writer, Tafolla performs scenes from her reminiscences on stage.*

I know when I began—or at least when I was born, on July 29th, 1951, at 8:41 P.M.—but that isn't really the whole story. My beginnings were somehow rooted in memories passed on to me through my grandmother's sayings and my father's songs, and my mother's stories, and in some mountains that I saw once from the highway, and in the thread of a dream below the voice and between the words of someone whose name I don't know but whose voice and dream I still carry.

The way I defined family was much like the old funerals I remember. In the front rows were the next of kin, the most greatly affected by the loss, behind them those close, behind them the friends, then the acquaintances and always, somewhere, the people of whom no one knew the exact relationship to the departed, but that didn't matter—those people knew, and that was enough reason to be there. In fact, one's own internal reasons were the guiding law for anyone's presence, and no one had to make explanations at a time like that. Modern "family sections" later served to cut off, to make people separate off, who was family from who wasn't, who was "immediate family" from who was "distant." None of this was necessary in the old Mexicano funerals I remembered. The cousin (*prima hermana*,[1] to emphasize how close the relationship really was) who'd spent eighty years of her life with the deceased didn't have to be turned away from the three skimpy rows of "Family Section" just in order to allow room for younger siblings and spouse, nieces and nephews, who'd only spent twenty to sixty-some-odd years with the deceased. There was no having to judge "degree" of relationship, in competition with the others present. One merely found one's place according to one's own intuition.

Family was like that. There was the little boy in second grade that I was proud to claim as my "third step cousin-in-law" and there were the friends for whom no blood connection existed, but who counted in every way as cousins, to whom there was a life-long commitment and a life-long connection.

It was a big family. It seemed I had several dozen aunts and uncles, and at least fifty of the immediate cousins. It was a context that provided variety and contrast. "Somos como los frijoles pintos," my grandmother would say, "algunos güeros, algunos morenos, y algunos con pecas." (We're like pinto beans in this family—some light, some dark, and some with freckles.) I knew my grandmother so well, through all her sayings,

---

[1] *prima hermana*—first cousin.

but these had been told to me by my father, years after her death. I knew her through my father, even the details of her death, a death that happened shortly after my first birthday. Still, she guides me through many days, telling me "No hay sábado sin sol ni domingo sin misa." (There's no Saturday that doesn't have some sunshine, no Sunday that doesn't have a Mass.) Still, she warms me "Díme con quien andas y te diré quien eres." (Tell me who you hang around with, and I'll tell you who you are.)

She was from Mexico, a proud, quiet woman, who spoke little and said much, whose skirts always touched the ground, who never raised her voice or lowered her sense of dignity. Her high cheekbones were echoed in my father's face and in my own. I find it hard to imagine her as a noisy child, as a noisy anything.

My grandfather, on the other hand, lived by words. Words were his tools, and he was a man who valued tools. "Cómprate un fierro con cada día de pago" (Buy yourself one tool every payday), he gave my father as *consejo*,[2] and he taught his sons carpentry, plumbing, construction, and a hunger to build things. My father would later teach me, perhaps more randomly than he would have constructed the lessons for a boy, but still I knew how to use a hammer and a drill, how to putty the nail holes and clean a carburetor,[3] and most importantly, how to hunger to build things. Had the training been less random, less riddled with gaps, I would have known *how* to build things. As it is, I sit with pen and paper today, and try to plan and guess how I could put together a table or a house, how to do it right, for it would not do to make one not solid, not *"macizo."*[4]

Yet my grandfather's main occupation in life was using words as tools. The preacher, teacher, leader, he

---

[2] *consejo*—advice.

[3] carburetor—engine device that mixes fuel and air.

[4] *"macizo"*—filled in.

was the first in the family (possibly in the whole barrio) to own a typewriter. I don't know how old he was when he got it, but it was still his, marked with his work and his determination, used solidly and squarely as any of his tools, the fountain of many letters, that somehow always looked as individual as if he'd marked them by fountain pen and fingerprint.

His name was Mariano Tafolla. It was his grandfather's name, my father's name, and my father's oldest brother's name. Searching through the Santa Fe archives a few years ago, I found his grandfather's signature. It was almost a duplicate of my father's. I keep the name Tafolla, although my signature, perhaps even my personality, is far different. Perhaps it has something to do with words. With finding your place in the old Mexicano funerals, by internal guide, by intuition. This is who I am.

I have always considered my life one of great fortune, and the barrio was one of these points of fortune. It was a place rich in story and magic, warmth and wisdom. So magic it was that even the police would not come there, despite calls or complaints, unless they came in twos, with their car doors locked. We played baseball in the streets, shot off firecrackers on the Fourth of July, and raised our Easter chicks to fully grown (and temporarily spoiled) chickens.

When I was, years later, to hear about slums and ghettos, cultural **deprivation**,[5] and poverty-warped childhoods—there was no identification in my mind with these. In our own view, we were wealthy—we had no deprivation of cultural experiences, but rather a double dose of *cultura*.[6] Yes, my Cousins from "up north" would come to visit, and they had so many more "facts" at hand, seemed to know so much and do so

---

[5] **deprivation**—loss.

[6] *cultura*—culture.

much in their schools. Our school had no interscholastic[7] activities, no spelling bees or science fairs, no playground equipment, nor even a fence.

The main thing the schools tried to teach us was not to speak Spanish. The main thing we learned was not to speak Spanish in front of the teachers, and not to lose Spanish within ourselves. Perhaps that is why so many good independent and critical minds came out of that time period. Or perhaps that is why so many good independent and critical minds dropped out of school. We learned—oh, did we learn, but it was not what the school district had planned for us to learn. It was much bigger than that.

We became filled with a hunger—I call it now, sometimes, Latino Hunger. A hunger to see ourselves, our families and friends, our values and lives and realities reflected in something other than our own minds. We wanted proof that we really existed—a proof documented in those many schoolbooks filled with Toms and Susans, and Dicks and Janes, but no Chuys or Guadalupes or Juanas, no Adelitas or Santos or Esperanzas. And we definitely needed Esperanzas,[8] if we were to dream of anything at all beyond the sirens, the friskings,[9] and the punishments for the sin of having spoken Spanish at school. There was a hunger and a place in our lives that needed to be filled with Esperanzas and Milagros.[10]

So what we didn't see, we invented. Even the national anthem became our cultural playground: "Jo—o—sé, can you see—ee?" And we filled TV with our own raza,[11] hidden between the lines and in the shadows of people's pasts.

---

[7] interscholastic—between schools or scholars.

[8] Esperanzas—*esperanza* means "hope" or "hopefulness."

[9] friskings—body searches.

[10] Milagros—miracles.

[11] *raza*—race; people.

My roots in New Mexico go back for centuries—
españoles[12] arriving in the 17th century to *indios parientes*[13]
already there. The move to Texas happened between
1848 and 1865 (a few wars got in the way, causing
strange demographic reshuffles). My great-great-grand-
mother was already there, and had a seamstress shop in
"downtown" San Antonio; my great-grandmother
washed clothes in the San Antonio River; her *tío*[14] had
brought word in 1836 to Juan Seguín and the *tejanos* at
the Alamo that Santa Ana's army was coming in great
force. (They didn't listen.) She later married two (one at a
time) Confederate veterans. Growing up, I teased that
I had relatives on all sides of all wars.

The Tafollas' roots were in New Mexico, the Salinas'
in San Antonio, the Sánchez' in Montemorelos,[15] the
Duartes' and Morenos' in Spain, but somehow it was
San Antonio that won out. San Antonio is in my blood.
Maybe that's because its earth was worn smooth by so
many first-step baby feet kissed by mothers before my
mother. Maybe because its air was charged by the anger
and tension and passion of fights between family members
and then warmed by the *abrazos*[16] between them, healing
their hearts. Maybe it's that the sunshine captured the
laughter, or the river collected the tears from my own
eyes and a thousand crying family eyes before me, and
then returned the same life-moisture in rain to celebrate,
and in honest sweat from good work done. Maybe it's
the softness of the grass, the softness of the earth, that
holds the softness of all those buried there by blood or
heart related: my grandparents, my aunts, my father, my

---

[12] *españoles*—Spaniards.

[13] *indios parientes*—Indian relatives.

[14] *tío*—uncle.

[15] Montemorelos—city in northeastern Mexico.

[16] *abrazos*—hugs.

first-born child, and a thousand cousins and cousins of cousins for centuries held together by the warmth of *familia*.

From the *vaqueros, rancheros, soldados,*[17] preachers, teachers and storytellers on my father's side and the metalworkers, maids, nursemaids, and servant people on my mother's side come the family members that sit by my side as I write today. So do the mesquite trees and *vacas*, coyotes and *ríos* of their lives, and the *molcajetes* and *gatos, libros*[18] and computers, friends and strangers, races, telephones and headlines—of mine. They are all a part of my *familia*, that huge network of creatures in coexistence, sharing places and times and feelings, sharing commitment, sharing care about each other. . .

But that only tells part of the story. Because we don't have photographs or even mental images of most of the people that form our *familia*—we don't even know who they were, or who they will be. And everything and everyone I see out there, and the even more numerous ones I don't see, are all the real members of my *familia*. And when we speak of family, who can we really leave out?

---

[17] *vaqueros, rancheros, soldados*—cowboys, ranchers, soldiers.

[18] *vacas, ríos, molcajetes, gatos, libros*—cows, rivers, mortar and pestle, cats, books.

QUESTIONS TO CONSIDER

1. From whom does the speaker believe she received her own family values?

2. What does the speaker mean when she says, "We became filled with a hunger—I call it now, sometimes, Latino Hunger"?

3. In Tafolla's opinion, what are some advantages of being from a big family?

Authors

▲
Ilan Stavans

Gary Soto ▶

Pablo Medina, right, raises his
hands with retired Lt. Col.
Francisco Cardenas of Mexico.
▼

Dagoberto Gilb ▶

Richard Rodriguez
▼

◀ Piri Thomas

Judith Ortíz Cofer
▼

▲
José Martí

Cesar Chavez ▶

Julia Alvarez wearing a shirt depicting Mexican Revolutionary hero, Emiliano Zapata.
▼

▲
Rafael Campo

Self

from

Hunger of Memory

BY RICHARD RODRIGUEZ

*Richard Rodriguez, born in 1947 to Mexican parents, grew up
in California. His* Hunger of Memory *was published in 1982. In
the memoir, Rodriguez looks back on his youth and his developing
sense of self, often reflecting on how language shapes a person's
experience. The book's attacks on affirmative action and bilingual
education immediately turned its author into a controversial figure.
Rodriguez works for PBS in "The News Hour with Jim Lehrer"
and is an editor at Pacific News Service. This excerpt is from
a section of his memoir entitled "Complexion."*

Visiting the East Coast or the gray capitals of Europe
during the long months of winter, I often meet people at
deluxe hotels who comment on my **complexion**.[1] (In
such hotels it appears nowadays a mark of leisure and
wealth to have a complexion like mine.) Have I been
skiing? In the Swiss Alps? Have I just returned from a

---

[1] **complexion**—skin color and texture.

Caribbean vacation? No. I say no softly but in a firm voice that intends to explain: My complexion is dark. (My skin is brown. More exactly, terra-cotta[2] in sunlight, tawny in shade. I do not redden in sunlight. Instead, my skin becomes progressively dark; the sun singes the flesh.)

When I was a boy the white summer sun of Sacramento would darken me so, my T-shirt would seem bleached against my slender dark arms. My mother would see me come up the front steps. She'd wait for the screen door to slam at my back. "You look like a *negrito*,"[3] she'd say, angry, sorry to be angry, frustrated almost to laughing, scorn. "You know how important looks are in this country. With *los gringos*[4] looks are all that they judge on. But you! Look at you! You're so careless!" Then she'd start in all over again. "You won't be satisfied till you end up looking like *los pobres*[5] who work in the fields, *los braceros*."[6]

(*Los braceros*: Those men who work with their *brazos*, their arms; Mexican nationals who were licensed to work for American farmers in the 1950s. They worked very hard for very little money, my father would tell me. And what money they earned they sent back to Mexico to support their families, my mother would add. *Los pobres*—the poor, the pitiful, the powerless ones. But paradoxically also powerful men. They were the men with brown-muscled arms I stared at in awe on Saturday mornings when they showed up downtown like gypsies to shop at Woolworth's or Penney's. On Monday nights they would gather hours early on the steps of the Memorial Auditorium for the wrestling matches. Passing by on my bicycle in summer, I would spy them there, clustered in small groups, talking—frightening

[2] terra-cotta—like brownish orange earthenware.
[3] *negrito*—little black person.
[4] *los gringos*—white Americans.
[5] *los pobres*—the poor.
[6] *los braceros*—day laborers.

and fascinating men—some wearing Texas *sombreros* and T-shirts which shone fluorescent in the twilight. I would sit forward in the back seat of our family's '48 Chevy to see them, working alongside Valley highways: dark men on an even horizon, loading a truck amid rows of straight green. Powerful, powerless men. Their fascinating darkness—like mine—to be feared.)

"You'll end up looking just like them."

* * *

Regarding my family, I see faces that do not closely resemble my own. Like some other Mexican families, my family suggests Mexico's confused colonial past. Gathered around a table, we appear to be from separate continents. My father's face recalls faces I have seen in France. His complexion is white—he does not tan; he does not burn. Over the years, his dark wavy hair has grayed handsomely. But with time his face has sagged to a perpetual sigh. My mother, whose surname is **inexplicably**[7] Irish—Moran—has an olive complexion. People have frequently wondered if, perhaps, she is Italian or Portuguese. And, in fact, she looks as though she could be from southern Europe. My mother's face has not aged as quickly as the rest of her body; it remains smooth and glowing—a cool tan—which her gray hair cleanly **accentuates**.[8] My older brother has inherited her good looks. When he was a boy people would tell him that he looked like Mario Lanza,[9] and hearing it he would smile with dimpled assurance. He would come home from high school with girl friends who seemed to me glamorous (because they were) blonds. And during those years I envied him his skin that burned red and peeled like the skin of the *gringos*. His complexion never darkened like mine. My youngest

---

[7] **inexplicably**—without explanation.

[8] **accentuates**—emphasizes.

[9] Mario Lanza—popular, handsome opera singer of the 1950s and 1960s.

sister is exotically pale, almost ashen. She is delicately featured, Near Eastern, people have said. Only my older sister has a complexion as dark as mine, though her facial features are much less harshly defined than my own. To many people meeting her, she seems (they say) Polynesian.[10] I am the only one in the family whose face is severely cut to the line of ancient Indian ancestors. My face is mournfully long, in the classical Indian manner; my profile suggests one of those beak-nosed Mayan sculptures—the eaglelike face upturned, open-mouthed, against the deserted, primitive sky.

"We are Mexicans," my mother and father would say, and taught their four children to say whenever we (often) were asked about our ancestry. My mother and father scorned those "white" Mexican-Americans who tried to pass themselves off as Spanish. My parents would never have thought of denying their ancestry. I never denied it: My ancestry is Mexican, I told strangers mechanically. But I never forgot that only my older sister's complexion was as dark as mine.

My older sister never spoke to me about her complexion when she was a girl. But I guessed that she found her dark skin a burden. I knew that she suffered for being a [derogatory term for African American]. As she came home from grammar school, little boys came up behind her and pushed her down to the sidewalk. In high school, she struggled in the adolescent competition for boyfriends in a world of football games and proms, a world where her looks were plainly uncommon. In college, she was afraid and scornful when dark-skinned foreign students from countries like Turkey and India found her attractive. She revealed her fear of dark skin to me only in adulthood when, regarding her own three children, she quietly admitted relief that they were all light.

---

[10] Polynesian—from a Pacific island.

That is the kind of remark women in my family have often made before. As a boy, I'd stay in the kitchen (never seeming to attract any notice), listening while my aunts spoke of their pleasure at having light children. (The men, some of whom were dark-skinned from years of working out of doors, would be in another part of the house.) It was the woman's spoken concern: the fear of having a dark-skinned son or daughter. Remedies were exchanged. One aunt prescribed to her sisters the **elixir**[11] of large doses of castor oil[12] during the last weeks of pregnancy. (The remedy risked an abortion.) Children born dark grew up to have their faces treated regularly with a mixture of egg white and lemon juice concentrate. (In my case, the solution never would take.[13]) One Mexican-American friend of my mother's, who regarded it a special blessing that she had a measure of English blood, spoke **disparagingly**[14] of her husband, a construction worker, for being so dark. "He doesn't take care of himself," she complained. But the remark, I noticed, annoyed my mother, who sat tracing an invisible design with her finger on the tablecloth.

There was affection too and a kind of humor about these matters. With daring tenderness, one of my uncles would refer to his wife as *mi negra*. An aunt regularly called her dark child *mi feito* (my little ugly one), her smile only partially hidden as she bent down to dig her mouth under his ticklish chin. And at times relatives spoke scornfully of pale, white skin. A *gringo's* skin resembled *masa*— baker's dough—someone remarked. Everyone laughed. Voices chuckled over the fact that the *gringos* spent so many hours in summer sunning themselves. ("They need to get sun because they look like *los muertos*.")[15]

---

[11] **elixir**—sweet medicine.

[12] castor oil—oily medicine used as a laxative.

[13] take—have the desired effect.

[14] **disparagingly**—belittlingly; showing disrespect for.

[15] *los muertos*—the dead.

I heard the laughing but remembered what the women had said, with unsmiling voices, concerning dark skin. Nothing I heard outside the house, regarding my skin, was so impressive to me.

In public I occasionally heard racial slurs. Complete strangers would yell out at me. A teenager drove past, shouting, "Hey, Greaser! Hey, Pancho!" Over his shoulder I saw the giggling face of his girl friend. A boy pedaled by and announced matter-of-factly, "I pee on dirty Mexicans." Such remarks would be said so casually that I wouldn't quickly realize that they were being addressed to me. When I did, I would be paralyzed with embarrassment, unable to return the insult. (Those times I happened to be with white grammar school friends, *they* shouted back. **Imbued**[16] with the mysterious kindness of children, my friends would never ask later why I hadn't yelled out in my own defense.)

In all, there could not have been more than a dozen incidents of name-calling. That there were so few suggests that I was not a primary victim of racial abuse. But that, even today, I can clearly remember particular incidents is proof of their impact. Because of such incidents, I listened when my parents remarked that Mexicans were often mistreated in California border towns. And in Texas. I listened carefully when I heard that two of my cousins had been refused admittance to an "all-white" swimming pool. And that an uncle had been told by some man to go back to Africa. I followed the progress of the southern black civil rights movement, which was gaining prominent notice in Sacramento's afternoon newspaper. But what most intrigued me was the connection between dark skin and poverty. Because I heard my mother speak so often about the **relegation**[17] of

---

[16] **Imbued**—Filled.

[17] **relegation**—assignment.

dark people to **menial**[18] labor, I considered the great victims of racism to be those who were poor and forced to do menial work. People like the farmworkers whose skin was dark from the sun.

After meeting a black grammar school friend of my sister's, I remember thinking that she wasn't really "black." What interested me was the fact that she wasn't poor. (Her well-dressed parents would come by after work to pick her up in a shiny green Oldsmobile.) By contrast, the garbage men who appeared every Friday morning seemed to me unmistakably black. (I didn't bother to ask my parents why Sacramento garbage men always were black. I thought I knew.) One morning I was in the backyard when a man opened the gate. He was an ugly, square-faced black man with popping red eyes, a pail slung over his shoulder. As he approached, I stood up. And in a voice that seemed to me very weak, I piped, "Hi." But the man paid me no heed. He strode past to the can by the garage. In a single broad movement, he overturned its contents into his larger pail. Our can came crashing down as he turned and left me watching, in awe.

"*Pobres negros*," my mother remarked when she'd notice a headline in the paper about a civil rights demonstration in the South. "How the *gringos* mistreat them." In the same tone of voice she'd tell me about the mistreatment her brother endured years before. (After my grandfather's death, my grandmother had come to America with her son and five daughters.) "My sisters, we were still all just teenagers. And since *mi pápa* was dead, my brother had to be the head of the family. He had to support us, to find work. But what skills did he have! Twenty years old. *Pobre*. He was tall, like your grandfather. And strong. He did construction work. 'Construction!' The *gringos* kept him digging all day,

---

[18] **menial**—servantlike.

doing the dirtiest jobs. And they would pay him next to nothing. Sometimes they promised him one salary and paid him less when he finished. But what could he do? Report them? We weren't citizens then. He didn't even know English. And he was dark. What chances could he have? As soon as we sisters got older, he went right back to Mexico. He hated this country. He looked so tired when he left. Already with a hunchback.[19] Still in his twenties. But old-looking. No life for him here. *Pobre.*"

* * *

Dark skin was for my mother the most important symbol of a life of oppressive labor and poverty. But both my parents recognized other symbols as well.

My father noticed the feel of every hand he shook. (He'd smile sometimes—marvel more than scorn—remembering a man he'd met who had soft, uncalloused hands.)

My mother would grab a towel in the kitchen and rub my oily face sore when I came in from playing outside. "Clean the *graza*[20] off of your face!" (*Greaser!*)

Symbols: When my older sister, then in high school, asked my mother if she could do light housework in the afternoons for a rich lady we knew, my mother was frightened by the idea. For several weeks she troubled over it before granting conditional permission: "Just remember, you're not a maid. I don't want you wearing a uniform." My father echoed the same warning. Walking with him past a hotel, I watched as he stared at a doorman dressed like a Beefeater.[21] "How can anyone let himself be dressed up like that? Like a clown. Don't you ever get a job where you have to put on a uniform." In summertime neighbors would ask me if I wanted to

---

[19] hunchback—abnormally humped back.

[20] *graza*—grease.

[21] Beefeater—British royal guard.

earn extra money by mowing their lawns. Again and again my mother worried: "Why did they ask *you*? Can't you find anything better?" Inevitably, she'd **relent**.[22] She knew I needed the money. But I was instructed to work after dinner. ("When the sun's not so hot.") Even then, I'd have to wear a hat. *Un sombrero de* baseball.

(*Sombrero.* Watching gray cowboy movies, I'd brood over the meaning of the broad-rimmed hat—that troubling symbol—which comically distinguished a Mexican cowboy from real cowboys.)

From my father came no warnings concerning the sun. His fear was of dark factory jobs. He remembered too well his first jobs when he came to this country, not intending to stay, just to earn money enough to sail on to Australia. (In Mexico he had heard too many stories of discrimination in *los Estados Unidos.*[23] So it was Australia, that distant island-continent, that loomed in his imagination as his "America.") The work my father found in San Francisco was work for the unskilled. A factory job. Then a cannery job. (He'd remember the noise and the heat.) Then a job at a warehouse. (He'd remember the dark stench of old urine.) At one place there were fistfights; at another a supervisor who hated Chinese and Mexicans. Nowhere a union.

His memory of himself in those years is held by those jobs. Never making money enough for passage to Australia; slowly giving up the plan of returning to school to **resume**[24] his third-grade education—to become an engineer. My memory of him in those years, however, is lifted from photographs in the family album which show him on his honeymoon with my mother— the woman who had convinced him to stay in America. I have studied their photographs often, seeking to find in those figures some clear resemblance to the man and

---

[22] **relent**—become less strict; give in.

[23] *los Estados Unidos*—the United States.

[24] **resume**—begin again.

the woman I've known as my parents. But the youthful faces in the photos remain, behind dark glasses, shadowy figures anticipating my mother and father.

They are pictured on the grounds of the Coronado Hotel near San Diego, standing in the pale light of a winter afternoon. She is wearing slacks. Her hair falls seductively over one side of her face. He appears wearing a double-breasted suit, an unneeded raincoat draped over his arm. Another shows them standing together, solemnly staring ahead. Their shoulders barely are touching. There is to their pose an aristocratic formality, an elegant Latin **hauteur**.[25]

The man in those pictures is the same man who was fascinated by Italian grand opera. I have never known just what my father saw in the spectacle, but he has told me that he would take my mother to the Opera House every Friday night—if he had money enough for orchestra seats.[26] ("Why go to sit in the balcony?") On Sundays he'd **don**[27] Italian silk scarves and a camel's hair coat to take his new wife to the polo matches in Golden Gate Park. But one weekend my father stopped going to the opera and polo matches. He would blame the change in his life on one job—a warehouse job, working for a large corporation which today advertises its products with the smiling faces of children. "They made me an old man before my time," he'd say to me many years later. Afterward, jobs got easier and cleaner. Eventually, in middle age, he got a job making false teeth. But his youth was spent at the warehouse. "Everything changed," his wife remembers. The **dapper**[28] young man in the old photographs yielded to the man I saw after dinner: **haggard**,[29] asleep on the sofa. During "The Ed

---

[25] **hauteur**—scornful pride; arrogance.

[26] orchestra seats—good seats on the main floor.

[27] **don**—put on.

[28] **dapper**—neatly dressed.

[29] **haggard**—worn out.

Sullivan Show" on Sunday nights, when Roberta Peters or Licia Albanese[30] would appear on the tiny blue screen, his head would jerk up alert. He'd sit forward while the notes of Puccini sounded before him. ("Un bel dí.")[31]

By the time they had a family, my parents no longer dressed in very fine clothes. Those symbols of great wealth and the reality of their lives too noisily clashed. No longer did they try to fit themselves, like paper-doll figures, behind trappings so foreign to their actual lives. My father no longer wore silk scarves or expensive wool suits. He sold his tuxedo to a second-hand store for five dollars. My mother sold her rabbit fur coat to the wife of a Spanish radio station disc jockey. ("It looks better on you than it does on me," she kept telling the lady until the sale was completed.) I was six years old at the time, but I recall watching the transaction with complete understanding. The woman I knew as my mother was already physically unlike the woman in her honeymoon photos. My mother's hair was short. Her shoulders were thick from carrying children. Her fingers were swollen red, toughened by housecleaning. Already my mother would admit to foreseeing herself in her own mother, a woman grown old, bald and bowlegged, after a hard lifetime of working.

In their manner, both my parents continued to respect the symbols of what they considered to be upper-class life. Very early, they taught me the *propria*[32] way of eating *como los ricos*.[33] And I was carefully taught elaborate formulas of polite greeting and parting. The dark little boy would be invited by classmates to the rich houses on Forty-fourth and Forty-fifth streets. "How do you do?" or

---

[30] Roberta Peters, Licia Albanese—opera singers.

[31] Puccini . . . "Un bel dí"—famous song from Giacomo Puccini's opera *Madame Butterfly*. "Un bel dí," in Italian, means "one fine day."

[32] *propria*—proper.

[33] *como los ricos*—like the rich.

"I am very pleased to meet you," I would say, bowing slightly to the amused mothers of classmates. "Thank you very much for the dinner; it was very delicious."

I made an impression. I intended to make an impression, to be invited back. (I soon realized that the trick was to get the mother or father to notice me.) From those early days began my association with rich people, my fascination with their secret. My mother worried. She warned me not to come home expecting to have the things my friends possessed. But she needn't have said anything. When I went to the big houses, I remembered that I was, at best, a visitor to the world I saw there. For that reason, I was an especially watchful guest. I was my parents' child. Things most middle-class children wouldn't trouble to notice, I studied. Remembered to see: the starched black and white uniform worn by the maid who opened the door; the Mexican gardeners—their complexions as dark as my own. (One gardener's face, glassed by sweat, looked up to see me going inside.)

"Take Richard upstairs and show him your electric train," the mother said. But it was really the vast polished dining room table I'd come to **appraise**.[34] Those nights when I was invited to stay for dinner, I'd notice that my friend's mother rang a small silver bell to tell the black woman when to bring in the food. The father, at his end of the table, ate while wearing his tie. When I was not required to speak, I'd skate the icy cut of crystal with my eye; my gaze would follow the golden threads etched onto the rim of china. With my mother's eyes I'd see my hostess's manicured nails and judge them to be marks of her leisure. Later, when my schoolmate's father would bid me goodnight, I would feel his soft fingers and palm when we shook hands. And turning to leave, I'd see my dark self, lit by chandelier light, in a tall hallway mirror.

---

[34] **appraise**—evaluate.

1. Why does Rodriguez say "Nothing I heard outside the house, regarding my skin, was so impressive to me"?

2. How have Rodriguez's experiences as a youth influenced his sense of self?

3. Based on this excerpt, what do you think is the author's opinion of his own worth as a human being?

What the Future Brings

BY GARY SOTO AND JIMMY SANTIAGO BACA

Gary Soto was born in 1952 in Fresno, California. He published four books of poetry and four books of prose in the 1990s alone. He now writes mostly for young adults and is increasingly involved in filmmaking.

Jimmy Santiago Baca (1952–   ) is an award-winning Chicano poet and political activist. His books include Martín & Meditations on the South Valley, *which won the 1988 American Book Award,* Black Mesa Poems, *and* Immigrants in Our Own Land. *Baca lives in New Mexico and is also a film writer.*

Brown Girl, Blonde Okie
by Gary Soto

Jackie and I cross-legged
In the yard, plucking at
Grass, cupping flies
And shattering them against
Each other's faces—
Smiling that it's summer,
No school, and we can
Sleep out under stars
And the blink of jets
Crossing up our lives.
The flies leave, or die,
And we are in the dark,
Still cross-legged,
Talking not dogs or baseball,
But whom will we love,
What brown girl or blonde
Okie to open up to
And say we are sorry
For our faces, the filth
We shake from our hair,
The teeth without direction.
"We're ugly," says Jackie
On one elbow, and stares
Lost between jets
At what this might mean.
In the dark I touch my
Nose, trace my lips, and pinch
My mouth into a dull flower.
Oh God, we're in trouble.

Fall

by Jimmy Santiago Baca

Somber hue diffused[1] on everything.
          Each creature, each emptied corn stalk,
          is richly bundled in mellow light.
In that open unharvested field of my own life,
I have fathered small joys and memories.
My heart was once a lover's swing that creaked in wind
of these calm fall days.
Autumn chants my visions to sleep,
and travels me back into a night
when I could touch stars and believed in myself. . . .

Along the way, grief broke me,
          my faith became hardened dirt
          walked over by too many people.
My heart now, as I walk down this dirt road,
on this calm fall day,
          is a dented
          tin bucket
          filled with fruits
          picked long ago.
          It's getting harder
          to lug the heavy bucket.
          I spill a memory on the ground,
          it gleams,
          rain on hot embers
          of yellow grass.

---

[1] Somber hue diffused—Gloomy color spread out.

QUESTIONS TO CONSIDER

1. How would you describe the speaker's attitude in Soto's poem?

2. How is color used differently in the two poems?

3. What kinds of "grief" do you think the speaker of Baca's poem has experienced?

4. In these poems, how do the speakers see their own futures?

Visions of Cuba II

BY RAFAEL CAMPO AND
EVANGELINA COSSÍO Y CISNEROS

Rafael Campo (1963–   ) is a doctor of Cuban descent. He practices internal medicine at Harvard Medical School and Beth Israel Deaconess Medical Center in Boston. His books include What the Body Told, The Poetry of Healing, *and* Diva *(1999), from which this poem comes. Campo's poem describes Cuba as a "New World" (western hemisphere) country with a mixture of identities.*

Evangelina Cossío y Cisneros was born in Puerto Príncipe, Cuba, in 1878, the daughter of a prominent freedom fighter who wanted to win independence from Spain. Her father was condemned to death for his beliefs, but Cossío y Cisneros was able to get his sentence changed to life in prison. Cossío y Cisneros was also imprisoned. Her case became an international issue. A newspaper reporter from the United States eventually helped Cossío y Cisneros escape, dressed as a man. She arrived in New York to a big public reception. Eventually, she wrote her autobiography, The Story of Evangelina Cisneros, *published in 1898, from which this segment is taken.*

The New World's History in Three Voices
by Rafael Campo

Confusing Cuba with a wealthy land,
Columbus started what for centuries
has plagued the people who survived in me:
part-slave, part-royalty, part-Caliban,[1]

cross-dresser[2] in the golden silk the sea
rolls out along a beach that isn't mine,
American yet un-American
because not one of us is truly free,

I am compelled to sing in rhyme
forgetting what the end of beauty is.
I know that beauty is both grand and wise;
I know that Cuba's dying is a crime

that started with Columbus and his lies.
The Caliban in me will dance as if
he understands that beauty is like love;
the royalty in me could do with less,

but always wants whatever he can have.
Today, I think I'm just as beautiful
as something I convince myself I feel
but can't remember, what the proud black slave

in me would call "the greatest gift of all."
I don't know what she means by that, her hands
so calloused none are more American,
but sing for this island, this miracle.

---

[1] Caliban—Twentieth-century Latino writers often saw Caliban, Shakespeare's wild, enslaved character from *The Tempest*, as the voice of the downtrodden native and black people of the Americas.

[2] cross-dresser—person who wears clothes usually worn by the opposite sex.

To Free Cuba

by Evangelina Cossío y Cisneros

This is the story of my life. American women may find it interesting. It is at least true. I am not used to writing, but will tell my story as well as I can. I will try to make everything plain and easy to understand, although it will be hard for any one who has never lived in Cuba to believe that some of the things which I must tell could really happen so close to the free country of America.

To begin with, I am not a girl, as all the people who have been writing about me always say I am. I am a woman. I am nineteen years old.

I was born in Puerto Principe. Puerto Principe is the capital of a Province of Camiguey. It is a little city, where there were many happy people before the Revolution.[3] Camiguey is said by Americans to be the Kentucky of Cuba. By that, I think, they mean that we have beautiful horses there, and that we are proud of the prettiest girls in Cuba. I am one of four sisters. My mother died before I can remember. They say she was a very little woman, and that she was exceedingly pretty. She had large eyes, and she was very slender, and she had the lightest foot in the dance of any girl in Camiguey. Her name was Caridad de Cisneros y Litorre. My father's name was Jose Augustine Cossío y Serrano. There were four of us children, all girls. Flor de Maria was the eldest. She it is who has told me so much about my mother. Then came Carmen and then Clemencia, and then I. We were all very happy when we lived in Camiguey. It was always warm and pleasant there, but sometimes the trade-wind blows, and then it is well to stay indoors.

We girls had a little garden, and it was our pleasure to make the flowers grow. Flor de Maria made it her

---

[3] the Revolution—Cuba's fight for independence from Spain beginning in the mid-1800s. That independence came with the conclusion of the Spanish-American War in 1898.

especial business to raise the beans and the peppers and the many things that we of Cuba like to eat. My father had a little money, and we lived in a pretty house with thick walls to keep out the sun, and a court, with a fountain in it, where all of us children learned to walk. That is the first thing I can remember, the fountain. It leaped and sparkled in the sun, and I used to think it was alive and try to catch it, and make it stand still and talk with me. When I was in prison I often dreamt of the fountain which danced so gayly in the little court-yard.

My father was a good man, and he loved his children. It was always a holiday for us when he came home. But he was never happy in Camiguey after my mother died. He thought first of going one place and then to another. He could not bear to stay in the little home where he first took her as a bride. So he sold it, and we went with him from one place to another all over our beautiful Cuba. At last we came to Sagua La Grande, a seaport on the north coast of the island. There we found an old friend who had known my mother when she was a little girl; Rafael Canto y Nores was his name. He took us to his house, and his good wife was like a mother to us. My father went to a large sugar plantation close by and became weighmaster[4] there, and for seven years I lived with Señora Nores. She was very good to me. By and by my father was sent for to come to Cienfuegos. Cienfuegos is on the south coast of Cuba, and there is an estate there which is the largest plantation on the island. It is called the Constancia estate. When he was settled at Constancia he sent for Carmen and me.

My other sisters stayed with Signora Nores.

My father had a pretty little house near the estate and Carmen and I kept it for him as well as we could. Señora Nores had taught me how to make *tortillas* and *arroz con pollo*[5] and all of the good Cuban dishes. We had

---

[4] weighmaster—person responsible for accurate measurements.

[5] *arroz con pollo*—chicken and rice.

a happy time there in our little house; for Carmen and me, and it was almost like playing in a doll's house.

But my father was a strange man in some ways. He would have been better pleased if one of his children had been a son. He often looked at me, and took my head between his hands and said to me, "Evangelina, when I look at your brow it seems to me that you should have been my son and not my daughter," and then I would laugh and put my hands at my sides and pretend to whistle, and my father would cover my mouth with his hand, for in Cuba it is not good for a young girl to behave as the boys behave.

But for all that my father treated me more like a son than like a daughter. In the evening, when he had finished his supper, and we sat together he would talk to me about his business and his work at the plantation, and he would tell me of the things which **vexed**[6] him, and of the things which had pleased him during the day. He talked much to me about Cuba, and many a time I have sat with my father until the moon arose, and listened to his stories of the ten-years' war against Spain,[7] until every drop of blood in my veins was afire with the love of my brave country. My father told me how he had kissed my mother good-bye. She did not even weep, as she stood at the window, waving her hand to him and crying "Viva Cuba!" while he went down the path—out to fight for his country. Often he told me how she used to write to him, and tell him of his children at home, and what they did and said, and of how she missed him and prayed for him; but always he said the letters ended with the words, "Viva Cuba!"

When he had told me these things his voice would be a little rough sometimes, and he would speak quick, and I knew that he was trying hard to keep from crying; then I always went and sat by him, and held his hand

---

[6] **vexed**—annoyed; puzzled.

[7] the ten-years' war against Spain—1868–1878.

against my face, and he told me that I had eyes like my mother's eyes—like hers!

In all these talks with my father he did not treat me as most Cuban fathers treat their daughters. He spoke to me freely and without reserve, and through him I knew something more of the world than most Cuban girls, who are brought up in the **seclusion**[8] of their homes, ever dream of knowing.

One day (it was in May, a very hot day in 1895) Carmen and I had prepared supper and my father came home at his usual hour.

He did not kiss me when he came into the house, and when we were at the table he sat a long time without speaking.

I knew that there was to be war in Cuba. My father had told me so. I had heard his friends sitting in the shadow of the house and talking to him about it. When he did not speak to me as usual that night I knew that something had happened. I wished to ask him what it was, but I was afraid. All at once he pushed away his plate, and jumped up from the table. He caught me by the shoulders and looked straight into my eyes.

"My little girl," he said, "I am going to fight for Cuba."

I put my arms round his neck and kissed him, and then, I think, I cried a little, and my father kissed me and did not speak.

"Father," I said, "I am going with you," and from that moment my father knew that my mind was made up.

He never tried to persuade me not to go. He told me again of my mother and of her courage and her devotion to the cause of Cuba, and of his young sister Soleded, who had fought by his side in the former war.

That night we sat late and talked of many things.

---

[8] **seclusion**—hidden isolation.

QUESTIONS TO CONSIDER

1. What are the three voices of the title of Campo's poem?

2. Why do you think Campo says "not one of us is truly free"?

3. How did her father influence Cossío y Cisneros's sense of herself?

4. Which of Campo's three voices do you think would most appeal to Cossío y Cisneros?

Farewell in Welfare Island

BY JULIA DE BURGOS

Julia de Burgos was born in Puerto Rico in 1914 and died in New York City in 1953. She was a feminist poet and an internationally recognized advocate of Puerto Rican independence, the topic of this poem. She also expressed strong antidictatorship views. Her works are considered a cornerstone of Puerto Rican and Latino poetry. Her complete poems were translated into English by Jack Agüeros.

Welfare Island, known today as Roosevelt Island, is part of Manhattan. In 1828, the city of New York built a prison and a workhouse on the island that quickly developed very bad reputations. These were replaced by city hospitals in 1934.

It has to be from here,
right this instance,
my cry into the world.

Life was somewhere forgotten
and sought refuge in depths of tears
and sorrows
over this vast empire of solitude
and darkness.

Where is the voice of freedom,
freedom to laugh,
to move
without the heavy phantom of despair?

Where is the form of beauty
unshaken in its veil simple and pure?
Where is the warmth of heaven
pouring its dreams of love in broken spirits?

It has to be from here,
right this instance,
my cry into the world.
My cry that is no more mine,
but hers and his forever,
the comrades of my silence,
the phantoms of my grave.

It has to be from here,
forgotten but unshaken,
among comrades of silence
deep into Welfare Island
my farewell to the world.

    Goldwater Memorial Hospital
    Welfare Island, NYC
    Feb., 1953

QUESTIONS TO CONSIDER

1. What are some examples of images or phrases in the poem that express a desire for independence?

2. In what ways is Puerto Rico like a person in this poem?

3. How does the history of "Welfare Island" compare to the speaker's idea of Puerto Rico?

A Conversation with Piri Thomas

ILAN STAVANS AND PIRI THOMAS

Piri Thomas was born in 1928 in New York City. His mother was Puerto Rican and his father was Afro-Cuban. As a youth he belonged to a gang, and in 1952 he was sentenced to seven years in prison for his part in an armed robbery. While in prison, Thomas earned his GED, converted to Islam, joined the black pride movement, and began to write. His quest for a place for himself in society is chronicled in the memoir Down These Mean Streets. *His other books include* Seven Long Times *and* Stories from El Barrio, *which critics have praised for its honesty and creative imagery. In this 1994 dialogue with Ilan Stavans, Thomas explores his racial and ethnic identity.*

IS: I would like to start with the topic of language. Would you reflect on your relationship between Spanish and English? What does the Spanish language mean to you and what does the English language mean to you? How close or far away are you from each of them? What do you feel for each of them?

PT: I remember with all my heart and soul the first words that I learned from Mami and Papi were all in Spanish but as I grew up I knew that I was not speaking Spanish from Galicia or Barcelona in Spain. I was speaking the Spanish that is spoken in Puerto Rico, which I call Puerto Rican Spanish, because we kept our **nuances**[1] and feelings and energies and words that came from Africa like *chevere*, which means great. We are a mixture of all those who conquered us over the centuries, taking our women with or without permission. We are a culmination of all that energy, but our spirit is as free as it was born to be. We are a conglomeration of manifestations.[2]

IS: And so Spanish is the language in which you expressed your first words.

PT: *Sí*, I began to go through the same process that everyone has undergone under the system, beginning with the Native Americans: the **assimilation**[3] process. I remember in my own childhood in the thirties being in this school and I could not understand what the teacher was saying so much because they spoke very fast sometimes and I could not catch the words. I'd lean over to my friend saying "*Jose, mire*,[4] what did the teacher say?" He would tell me and I would continue to do my homework. And so that teacher came roaring upon me and said "listen, stop talking in that language," and I said "well, I am speaking my mother's language. My mother's from Puerto Rico, I was born in this country," and she says "well you stop talking that, you have to learn English, you are in America now. After

---

[1] **nuances**—slight differences in meaning.

[2] conglomeration of manifestations—collection of signs of existence.

[3] **assimilation**—transformation (to become a part of mainstream U.S. society).

[4] *mire*—look.

all, how else do you expect to become President of the United States if you do not learn to speak English correctly." I thought in my young heart, "my God this teacher has more faith than I have in my someday becoming President of the United States if I learn my English well enough." And the tremendous assimilation happened to me. As a child, I first had to think in Spanish to speak in English. Then, I had to think in English to speak in Spanish, because I had forgotten the language. I had forgotten the lessons that were taught in my home where my mother taught me how to read, beginning with readings from the Bible. So I've made a determined effort to regain my inheritance back to where I came from, to learn where I had come from in order to know where I was going, to be able to then recognize my true reality, the true reality of what we are in the scheme of things. I learned that we are human beings, but that there were those who believed that there were only two kinds of people on this earth: those who ruled and those who were ruled.

IS: But while we can reclaim our past through the Spanish language, we must acknowledge that Spanish is also the language used by the *conquistadores* in the Americas.

PT: I'm with you totally. In fact, I said it's **ironic**,[5] that we who are from all the *pueblos*,[6] Chile, Nicaragua, Peru, Ecuador, Cuba, Santo Domingo, Puerto Rico, all the islands, Central and South America, Mexico, are bound, blended, and held together by the language of the conqueror, whose fever for gold destroyed us physically, mentally, spiritually, and morally. They stripped away the **indigenous**[7] knowledge and the

---

[5] **ironic**—unexpected.

[6] *pueblos*—nations.

[7] **indigenous**—native; belonging to the first people to inhabit a place.

religious beliefs of those they found and forced everybody into their mold which was slavery.

IS: When you talk about regaining one's own past, one's own background and heritage, you seem to **imply**[8] that the way to do it is through language. I recently talked to a couple of Puerto Rican writers who are close friends and they were complaining that because they write in English in this country and are mainland Puerto Ricans, their work is almost totally ignored in the island because of the language issues. How about you? What is your situation? Is your work known in Puerto Rico?

PT: Well let me tell you, my brother, with all sincerity I agree. I went into San German,[9] I believe, where I met beautiful people. When I walked into the lobby, the walls were covered with photographs, beautiful photographs, of all the Puerto Rican brothers and sisters, writers, poets, and all the feelings and all the energies of a Luis Pales Matos or a Julia Burgos.[10] I looked to the walls for a picture of all of us from the Barrio and did not find one. So I asked the brother, "Why don't we have pictures of the poets and writers, brothers and sisters from *El Barrio*? Aren't we all *puertorriqueños*?"[11] And he told me "Well, because you don't write in Spanish." I told him "and what about these writers who wrote in French? These ones write in French, this one could speak German" and he just looked. I added "you have to remember one of our national poets Antonio Correrjer, who said that no matter if we're born on the moon we are still *puertorriqueños* to our soul." And "*nadie,*

---

[8] **imply**—suggest indirectly.

[9] San German—town in southwestern Puerto Rico.

[10] Luis Pales Matos, Julia Burgos—distinguished Puerto Rican poets, both of whom died in the 1950s.

[11] *puertorriqueños*—Puerto Ricans.

nobody," I told him, "can take away my heritage, because I, Juan Pedro Tomas, was born from a Puerto Rican womb, *boricua*. Although I was born in *el norte* my soul is Puerto Rican." But things are so mixed up for Puerto Ricans. The only reason why I knew of Puerto Rico is because I sat in the corner and listened to the grown-ups speaking about places like Fajardo, Bayamon, and San Juan,[12] among other places on the island. My beautiful child energy absorbed all that information by **osmosis**.[13] I finally went to Puerto Rico when I got out of prison at the age of thirty-two. My God, as that wall of green humidity enveloped me, it was like I was entering into my mother's arms. However, soon I began to see the reality of U.S. colonialism in Puerto Rico—a so-called Commonwealth, that really means common for the pueblo and wealth for the latter-day carpetbaggers[14] who enjoy a favorable tax status with the U.S. government.

IS: Let's focus on religion.

PT: I am a spiritual man. We all have a spirit—good, bad, or indifferent. I come from a family of different **denominations**.[15] My father was a deathbed Catholic. He was only going to see a priest when he was ready to kick the bucket, but he was a very good man, he did not drink, he did not smoke, he was a good athlete. He believed in doing unto others as you would like to be done to yourself. My lovely mother was a Seventh-Day Adventist, she cooked on Friday before the sun went down and

---

[12] Fajardo, Bayamon, San Juan—cities on the northeast coast of Puerto Rico; San Juan is the capital.

[13] **osmosis**—gradual internalization.

[14] carpetbaggers—Northerners who went to the South after the Civil War, seeking financial or political gain; here, wealthy newcomers from the United States.

[15] **denominations**—organized religious groups.

did not cook again until Saturday when the sun went down. We went to church on the Sabbath, we were the closest thing to the children of Israel in that sense of being. And my aunt, Angelita, my mother's sister, she was Pentecostal and I loved that church the best because you could express yourself there, with loud *Alleluias* and *Glorias a Dios*. In the others, you had to stay very quiet. In the Catholic church they spoke in Latin and I could not understand. But in the Pentecostal church, I could express myself. I began to think about God and what God was. I could not see him but they told me I could feel him, but that changed as the years went on and I made my inner journey, especially when I went to prison where you have plenty of time. I was determined that I was going to educate my mind. I was not going to **eradicate**[16] it. I made inner journeys within myself, so as to judge for myself on who I was in my sense of being. I wrote it into my poetry, "To me God is a smile on the face of a child that is not being wasted." "To me God is spelled G-O-O-D, good." Every child has their own gift of energy that can make direct contact with the power force within them as well as contact with others. Everything in life has had some kind of influence on me, in one way or another. In prison, I spent time reading books on the religions of Islam, Buddhism, Confucianism. I was looking for answers in my six-by-eight-by-nine prison cell.

IS: When did literature become an answer to you, a tool for salvation? Was it in prison, as you suggest at the end of *Down These Mean Streets*? Or was it before?

PT: Long before prison. My mother had saved some money from the sewing machine, because she used to work in the sweat shops but she also used to bring

---

[16] **eradicate**—completely get rid of.

home work from the job and work until two or three o'clock in the morning, because there was no work for my father. My father came running home one day happy, because he had hit the *bolita*, where you play *los números*—get three numbers and you win. And with that money and what my mother had saved we moved to a foreign country called Babylon, Long Island. I went to school out there, which became a battleground for me. I was the only little coffee grain for miles around in a sea of white milk. However, I had an English teacher, whose name was Mrs. Wright. She was very kind to me, this beautiful white teacher, and I loved her energy flows. One day she asked the class to write a composition about anything we wished. And I wrote a composition on how much I loved her beautiful brunette hair and her hazel eyes and how I loved the way she smelled when she came over to look at my work. However, I did not particularly care for her pronouns and adjectives and verbs because I did not know what the hell she was talking about. Then, days later, the papers came back and she asked me to turn mine over. I'd written two and a half pages; on the half-page that was left, it said in red pencil—I remember it to this day—"Son, your punctuation is lousy. Your grammar is non-existent. However, if you wish to be a writer someday, you will be. P.S. We both love my wife," signed her husband. Someone had recognized that I had a gift, an ability to express, to share feelings through words. I believe all children are born poets and that every poet is the child and what the children need is a world that will guide them towards creativity and not towards greed.

IS: Was there ever any writer while you were at that time in Babylon or later on while you were in jail that influenced you, not in terms of the friendship that you had with her or with him, but whose book you thought was something to **emulate**?[17]

PT: I loved to read as a kid. The reason I loved to read was because I was introduced by a very caring teacher to a very caring librarian on 110th Street in my Barrio. She allowed me to take out two books and I would go to the fire escape and turn my blanket into a hammock and I'd just sit back reading. I'd read whatever I found. I loved adventure stories, I loved science fiction or traveling to other universes. I loved the energies of Jack London and the white wolf and fang,[18] everything, the feelings. Actually, I didn't have a whole lot of time to read until I went to prison, where I found out that I could create a world in my mind that would take me away from all that if I really tuned myself to books and my imagination. One night, a brother whose nickname was Young Blood knocked on my prison cell. He knocked very low and I said "Aha" and he said "Tommy, Tommy, they wrote a book with my name on it, Young Blood, you know, and, man, I want you to read it. It's by a brother man, a black brother." At that time, we were calling each other black. And he handed me the book through the bars and it was called *Youngblood* by John Oliver Killens. He was an attorney who was also a very fine writer, a beautiful black human being. I read the book; it had been read by so many people that the pages were like onion skin. When I finished reading it, Young Blood asked, "what'd you think of it, Tommy?" and I said "Man, it was really dynamite, you live it, the whole feeling." And I added "Young Blood, you want to know something?" and he said "yeah" and I said, "I could write too." And he smiled at me and he said "yeah I know

---

[17] **emulate**—strive to be like.

[18] American author Jack London wrote several Alaskan adventure novels that show how people and animals adapt to the wilderness; one is entitled *White Fang*.

you can, Tommy" and that's when I began to write what would one day be known as *Down These Mean Streets*. At that time, it was entitled *Home Sweet Harlem*.

IS: I've heard you say that literature is useful to fight racism. But how effective can it be? Writers are also depressive types. Whenever they realize that words are simply words—**ephemeral**,[19] transient—they fall into an impossible **abyss**[20] of fatalism.[21]

PT: Words are important because they awaken consciousness and thus can inspire action. So you have to be careful how you use words because they can be bullets or butterflies. Children become what they learn or don't learn. Children become what they are taught or not taught. For thousands of years we have heard propaganda about white supremacy[22] and "might makes right." Because if you conquer people by might, strip away their education, their beliefs, their culture, and their land, then in two or three generations their children will be in the dark ages again. We had very bright minds when we first went into their schools, because children are not born stupid. The world has no right to judge intelligence by the color of one's skin. Different colors were meant to be very beautiful just like flowers come in different and beautiful colors. Birds are different colors. And this is the struggle that we have had to wage, to allow all the colors to express their humanity through literature and the other arts to learn from each other, as a people, for we are not only geographic locations, colors, sexes,

---

[19] **ephemeral**—short-lived.

[20] **abyss**—deep hole.

[21] fatalism—belief that all events are determined by fate and so cannot be changed.

[22] white supremacy—belief that light-skinned people deserve to have power over all others.

or preferences. We are earthlings who share a common bond—our humanity.

IS: When *Down These Mean Streets* came out, there was an immediate uproar in terms of the sexual **explicitness**[23] and there were even some legal problems. When you were writing the subsequent books, *Savior, Savior*, and *Seven Long Times*, and *Stories From El Barrio*, did the experience of the censorship with *Down These Mean Streets* affect you in any conscious or unconscious way when you were writing? Were you trying, in a sense, to be more defiant and explicit or less defiant and explicit?

PT: I didn't have too much time to think about all that. I was so **elated**[24] with my gift of being able to write even though the first book had almost killed me because it was such an outpouring—I almost suffered an emotional burnout. I could not stand the agony anymore. So when I wrote *Savior, Savior, Hold my Hand*, I wrote it more gentle. And when I wrote *Seven Long Times*, I was looking at it twenty-five years later, very objectively, like a scientist. But *Down These Mean Streets*, that was an explosion from my very soul and I will utilize part of that power in my upcoming book, *A Matter of Dignity*. I will have to go back to that time to relive it. Then, as my clarity of mind begins to rise, you will see that instead of rage without reason, there is now reason.

IS: *Down These Mean Streets* **inaugurated**[25] a new awareness.

PT: Everywhere I go, people congratulate me. Over the years I've received hundreds if not thousands of letters. People have said to me, "Bro, I had never read

---

[23] **explicitness**—detailed clarity.

[24] **elated**—filled with joy.

[25] **inaugurated**—formally began.

a book in my life but this was put in my hand and it opened my soul to reading. I never finished a book in my life, hey, bro, wow!" I was writing the rage out of me but at the same time, I was writing for all of us who were living in that hell. I was not born a criminal from my mother's womb, none of us who had been into the so-called criminal activity had been born criminals from our mother's womb. We were all born very beautiful children, just like any other little babies, into a very criminal society of racism and bigotry and horror to the nth degree, not to leave out promises that very rarely, if ever, came to be. Many people do not understand that to write that book I almost blew my mind. Because I had to force myself to go back in time and feel all the feelings again which included all the agony and the pain. That book was supposed to be something to be swept under the rug and forgotten but I went and opened Pandora's Box,[26] and out came not only the demons, but also the truths. That's why I could not leave a chapter unfinished; I would work on it three or four days straight, reliving all the emotions from that time. But once I discovered that the truth brought relief from the pain, it was wonderful. I then added humor and when you have humor you can laugh, and when you can laugh, the demons go away.

[26] Pandora's Box—mythical container full of evils.

QUESTIONS TO CONSIDER

1. What does Thomas mean when he says "I was the only little coffee grain for miles around in a sea of white milk"?

2. What happened to Thomas when someone recognized that he had a gift?

3. How has religion helped Thomas become who he is today?

4. Why did writing his book dramatically change Thomas's life?

from

. . . And the Earth Did Not Devour Him

BY TOMÁS RIVERA

Tomás Rivera (1935–1984) was born in Crystal City, Texas. He received a doctorate from the University of Oklahoma. His classic novel . . . And the Earth Did Not Devour Him, published in Spanish in 1971, is about migrant workers from Mexico in the southwestern United States. It has been translated into English and was also turned into a PBS movie. The following segment was translated by Evangelina Vigil-Piñón. The character being described is a young man coming of age in a family of migrant workers.

The first time he felt hate and anger was when he saw his mother crying for his uncle and his aunt. They both had caught tuberculosis and had been sent to different sanitariums.[1] So, between the brothers and sisters, they had split up the children among themselves and had

---

[1] sanitariums—health facilities for victims of diseases that take a long time to cure.

taken care of them as best they could. Then the aunt died, and soon thereafter they brought the uncle back from the sanitarium, but he was already spitting blood. That was when he saw his mother crying every little while. He became angry because he was unable to do anything against anyone. Today he felt the same. Only today it was for his father.

"You all should've come home right away, m'ijo.[2] Couldn't you see that your Daddy was sick? You should have known that he'd suffered a **sunstroke**.[3] Why didn't you come home?"

"I don't know. Us being so soaked with sweat, we didn't feel so hot, but I guess that when you're sunstruck it's different. But I did tell him to sit down under the tree that's at the edge of the rows, but he didn't want to. And that was when he started throwing up. Then we saw he couldn't hoc anymore and we dragged him and put him under a tree. He didn't put up a fuss at that point. He just let us take him. He didn't even say a word."

"Poor viejo,[4] my poor viejo. Last night he hardly slept. Didn't you hear him outside the house. He squirmed in bed all night with cramps. God willing, he'll get well. I've been giving him cool lemonade all day, but his eyes still look glassy. If I'd gone to the fields yesterday, I tell you, he wouldn't have gotten sick. My poor viejo, he's going to have cramps all over his body for three days and three nights at the least. Now, you all take care of yourselves. Don't overwork yourselves so much. Don't pay any mind to that boss if he tries to rush you. Just don't do it. He thinks it's so easy since he's not the one who's out there stooped."

He became even angrier when he heard his father moan outside the chicken coop. He wouldn't stay inside because he said it made him feel very anxious. Outside

---

[2] m'ijo—my little one.

[3] **sunstroke**—illness caused by too much heat.

[4] viejo—old man.

where he could feel the fresh air was where he got some relief. And also when the cramps came he could roll over on the grass. Then he thought about whether his father might die from the sunstroke. At times he heard his father start to pray and ask for God's help. At first he had faith that he would get well soon, but by the next day he felt the anger growing inside of him. And all the more when he heard his mother and his father clamoring for God's mercy. That night, well past midnight, he had been awakened by his father's groans. His mother got up and removed the scapularies[5] from around his neck and washed them. Then she lit some candles. But nothing happened. It was like his aunt and uncle all over again.

"What's to be gained from doing all that, Mother? Don't tell me you think it helped my aunt and uncle any. How come we're like this, like we're buried alive? Either the germs eat us alive or the sun burns us up. Always some kind of sickness. And every day we work and work. For what? Poor Dad, always working so hard. I think he was born working. Like he says, barely five years old and already helping his father plant corn. All the time feeding the earth and the sun, only to one day, just like that, get struck down by the sun. And there you are, helpless. And them, begging for God's help . . . why, God doesn't care about us . . . I don't think there even is . . . No, better not say it, what if Dad gets worse. Poor Dad, I guess that at least gives him some hope."

His mother noticed how furious he was, and that morning she told him to calm down, that everything was in God's hands and that with God's help his father was going to get well.

"Oh, Mother, do you really believe that? I am certain that God has no concern for us. Now you tell me, is Dad evil or mean-hearted? You tell me if he has ever done any harm to anyone."

---

[5] scapularies—sleeveless garments that cover the shoulders.

"Of course not."

"So there you have it. You see? And my aunt and uncle? You explain. And the poor kids, now orphans, never having known their parents. Why did God have to take them away? I tell you, God could care less about the poor. Tell me, why must we live here like this? What have we done to deserve this? You're so good and yet you have to suffer so much."

"Oh, please, m'ijo, don't talk that way. Don't speak against the will of God. Don't talk that way, please, m'ijo. You scare me. It's as if already the blood of Satan[6] runs through your veins."

"Well, maybe. That way at least, I could get rid of this anger. I'm so tired of thinking about it. Why? Why you? Why Dad? Why my uncle? Why my aunt? Why their kids? Tell me, Mother, why? Why us, burrowed in[7] the dirt like animals with no hope for anything? You know the only hope we have is coming out here every year. And like you yourself say, only death brings rest. I think that's the way my aunt and uncle felt and that's how Dad must feel too."

"That's how it is, m'ijo. Only death brings us rest."

"But why us?"

"Well, they say that . . ."

"Don't say it. I know what you're going to tell me— that the poor go to heaven."

That day started out cloudy and he could feel the morning coolness brushing his eyelashes as he and his brothers and sisters began the day's labor. Their mother had to stay home to care for her husband. Thus, he felt responsible for hurrying on his brothers and sisters. During the morning, at least for the first few hours, they endured the heat but by ten-thirty the sun had suddenly cleared the skies and pressed down against the world. They began working more slowly because of the

---

[6] Satan—the devil.

[7] burrowed in—dug into.

weakness, dizziness and suffocation they felt when they worked too fast. Then they had to wipe the sweat from their eyes every little while because their vision would get blurred.

"If you start blacking out, stop working, you hear me? Or go a little slower. When we reach the edge we'll rest a bit to get our strength back. It's gonna be hot today. If only it'd stay just a bit cloudy like this morning, then nobody would complain. But no, once the sun bears down like this not even one little cloud dares to appear out of fear. And the worst of it is we'll finish up here by two and then we have to go over to that other field that's nothing but hills. It's okay at the top of the hill but down in the lower part of the slopes it gets to be real suffocating. There's no breeze there. Hardly any air goes through. Remember?"

"Yeah."

"That's where the hottest part of the day will catch us. Just drink plenty of water every little while. It don't matter if the boss gets mad. Just don't get sick. And if you can't go on, tell me right away, all right? We'll go home. Y'all saw what happened to Dad when he pushed himself too hard. The sun has no mercy, it can eat you alive."

Just as they had figured, they had moved on to the other field by early afternoon. By three o'clock they were all soaked with sweat. Not one part of their clothing was dry. Every little while they would stop. At times they could barely breathe, then they would black out and they would become fearful of getting sunstruck, but they kept on working.

"How do y'all feel?"

"Man, it's so hot! But we've got to keep on. 'Til six, at least. Except this water don't help our thirst any. Sure wish I had a bottle of cool water, real cool, fresh from the well, or a coke ice-cold."

"Are you crazy? That'd sure make you sunsick right now. Just don't work so fast. Let's see if we can make it until six. What do you think?"

At four o'clock the youngest became ill. He was only nine years old, but since he was paid the same as a grown-up he tried to keep up with the rest. He began vomiting. He sat down, then he lay down. Terrified, the other children ran to where he lay and looked at him. It appeared that he had fainted and when they opened his eyelids they saw his eyes were rolled back. The next youngest child started crying, but right away he told him to stop and help him carry his brother home. It seemed he was having cramps all over his little body. He lifted him and carried him by himself and, again, he began asking himself *why?*

"Why Dad and then my little brother? He's only nine years old. Why? He has to work like a mule buried in the earth. Dad, Mom, and my little brother here, what are they guilty of?"

Each step that he took toward the house resounded with the question, *why?* About halfway to the house he began to get furious. Then he started crying out of rage. His little brothers and sisters did not know what to do, and they, too, started crying, but out of fear. Then he started cursing. And without even realizing it, he said what he had been wanting to say for a long time. He cursed God. Upon doing this he felt that fear instilled in him by the years and by his parents. For a second he saw the earth opening up to devour him. Then he felt his footsteps against the earth, compact, more solid than ever. Then his anger swelled up again and he **vented**[8] it by cursing God. He looked at his brother, he no longer looked sick. He didn't know whether his brothers and sisters had understood the graveness of his curse.

That night he did not fall asleep until very late. He felt at peace as never before. He felt as though he had become detached from everything. He no longer worried about his father nor his brother. All that he awaited was

[8] **vented**—expressed.

the new day, the freshness of the morning. By daybreak his father was doing better. He was on his way to recovery. And his little brother, too; the cramps had almost completely **subsided**.[9] Frequently he felt a sense of surprise upon recalling what he had done the previous afternoon. He thought of telling his mother, but he decided to keep it secret. All he told her was that the earth did not devour anyone, nor did the sun.

He left for work and encountered a very cool morning. There were clouds in the sky and for the first time he felt capable of doing and undoing anything that he pleased. He looked down at the earth and kicked it hard and said:

"Not yet, you can't swallow me up yet. Someday, yes. But I'll never know it."

---

[9] **subsided**—lessened.

QUESTIONS TO CONSIDER

1. How do the young man's experiences affect his faith in God?

2. Why do the people in this story work until they become ill?

3. How do you think the young man's anger influenced his self-esteem?

The Hammon and the Beans

BY AMÉRICO PAREDES

Américo Paredes (1915–1999) grew up in Brownsville, Texas, on the U.S.–Mexican border. In 1934, a poem he wrote won a state contest, and he began his career as a writer and educator. His scholarly work and most of his writings focus on the culture of the border. He won many awards, including the Oren del Aguila Azteca (Order of the Aztec Eagle), Mexico's highest honor for scholars from other countries. The Hammon and the Beans and Other Stories *was published in 1994.*

Once we lived in one of my grandfather's houses near Fort Jones. It was just a block from the parade grounds,[1] a big frame house painted a dirty yellow. My mother hated it, especially because of the pigeons that cooed all day about the **eaves**.[2] They had fleas, she said. But it was a quiet neighborhood at least, too far from the

---

[1] parade grounds—area where military troops assemble for review.

[2] **eaves**—projecting overhangs of the lower edge of a roof.

center of town for automobiles and too near for musical, night-roaming drunks.

At that time Jonesville-on-the-Grande was not the thriving little city that it is today. We told off our days by the routine on the post. At six sharp the flag was raised on the parade grounds to the cackling of the bugles, and a field piece[3] thundered out a salute. The sound of the shot bounced away through the morning mist until its echoes worked their way into every corner of town. Jonesville-on-the-Grande woke to the cannon's roar, as if to battle, and the day began.

At eight the whistle from the post laundry sent us children off to school. The whole town stopped for lunch with the noon whistle, and after lunch everybody went back to work when the post laundry said that it was one o'clock, except for those who could afford to be old-fashioned and took the siesta.[4] The post was the town's clock, you might have said, or like some insistent elder person who was always there to tell you it was time.

At six the flag came down, and we went to watch through the high wire fence that divided the post from the town. Sometimes we joined in the ceremony, standing at salute until the sound of the cannon made us jump. That must have been when we had just studied about George Washington in school, or recited "The Song of Marion's Men," about Marion the Fox[5] and the British cavalry that chased him up and down the broad Santee.[6] But at other times we stuck out our tongues and jeered at the soldiers. Perhaps the night before we had hung at the edges of a group of old men and listened to tales about Aniceto Pizaña[7] and the "border troubles," as the

---

[3] field piece—battleground weapon.

[4] siesta—rest after the midday meal.

[5] Marion the Fox—Francis Marion, a heroic guerrilla fighter in the American Revolutionary War.

[6] Santee—river in South Carolina.

[7] Aniceto Pizaña—hero, celebrated in *corridos* ("ballads"), for leading a revolt to create a Spanish-speaking republic in south Texas in 1915.

local paper still called them when it referred to them gingerly in passing.

It was because of the border troubles, ten years or so before, that the soldiers had come back to old Fort Jones. But we did not hate them for that; we admired them even, at least sometimes. But when we were thinking about the border troubles instead of Marion the Fox, we hooted them and the flag they were lowering, which for the moment was theirs alone, just as we would have jeered an opposing ball team, in a friendly sort of way. On these occasions even Chonita would join in the mockery, though she usually ran home at the stroke of six. But whether we **taunted**[8] or saluted, the distant men in khaki uniforms went about their motions without noticing us at all.

The last word from the post came in the night when a distant bugle blew. At nine it was all right because all the lights were on. But sometimes I heard it at eleven, when everything was dark and still, and it made me feel that I was all alone in the world. I would even doubt that I was me, and that put me in such a fright that I felt like yelling out just to make sure I was really there. But next morning the sun shone and life began all over again, with its whistles and cannon shots and bugles blowing. And so we lived, we and the post, side by side with the wire fence in between.

The wandering soldiers whom the bugle called home at night did not wander in our neighborhood, and none of us ever went into Fort Jones. None except Chonita. Every evening when the flag came down she would leave off playing and go down toward what was known as the lower gate of the post, the one that opened not on Main Street but against the poorest part of town. She went into the grounds and to the mess halls and pressed her nose against the screens and watched the soldiers eat. They sat at long tables calling to each other through food-stuffed mouths.

---

[8] **taunted**—jeered.

"Hey bud, pass the coffee!"

"Give me the ham!"

"Yeah, give me the beans!"

After the soldiers were through, the cooks came out and scolded Chonita, and then they gave her packages with things to eat.

Chonita's mother did our washing in gratefulness—as my mother put it—for the use of a vacant lot of my grandfather's which was a couple of blocks down the street. On the lot was an old one-room shack which had been a shed long ago, and this Chonita's father had patched up with flattened-out pieces of tin. He was a laborer. Ever since the end of the border troubles there had been a development boom[9] in the Valley, and Chonita's father was getting his share of the good times. Clearing brush and building irrigation ditches, he sometimes pulled down as much as six dollars a week. He drank a good deal of it up, it was true. But corn was just a few cents a bushel in those days. He was the breadwinner, you might say, while Chonita furnished the luxuries.

Chonita was a poet, too. I had just moved into the neighborhood when a boy came up to me and said, "Come on! Let's go hear Chonita make a speech."

She was already on top of the alley fence when we got there, a scrawny little girl of about nine, her bare dirty feet clinging to the fence almost like hands. A dozen other kids were there below her, waiting. Some were boys I knew at school; five or six were her younger brothers and sisters.

"Speech! Speech!" they all cried. "Let Chonita make a speech! Talk in English, Chonita!"

They were grinning and nudging each other, except for her brothers and sisters, who looked up at her with proud, serious faces. She gazed out beyond us all with a grand, distant air and then she spoke.

---

[9] development boom—rapid growth of population and construction.

"Give me the hammon[10] and the beans!" she yelled. "Give me the hammon and the beans!"

She leaped off the fence and everybody cheered and told her how good it was and how she could talk English better than the teachers at the grammar school.

I thought it was a pretty poor joke. Every evening almost, they would make her get up on the fence and yell, "Give me the hammon and the beans!" And everybody would cheer and make her think she was talking English. As for me, I would wait there until she got it over with so we could play at something else. I wondered how long it would be before they got tired of it all. I never did find out, because just about that time I got the chills and fever, and when I got up and around, Chonita wasn't there anymore.

In later years I thought of her a lot, especially during the thirties when I was growing up. Those years would have been just made for her. Many's the time I have seen her in my mind's eye, on the picket lines demanding not bread, not cake, but the hammon and the beans. But it didn't work out that way.

One night Doctor Zapata came into our kitchen through the back door. He set his bag on the table and said to my father, who had opened the door for him, "Well, she is dead."

My father flinched. "What was it?" he asked.

The doctor had gone to the window and he stood with his back to us, looking out toward the light of Fort Jones. "Pneumonia, flu, malnutrition, worms, the evil eye," he said without turning around. "What the hell difference does it make?"

"I wish I had known how sick she was," my father said in a very mild tone. "Not that it's really my affair, but I wish I had."

The doctor snorted and shook his head.

---

[10] hammon—in the Spanish word for ham, *jamón*, the first letter is pronounced like the English *h*.

My mother came in and I asked her who was dead. She told me. It made me feel strange but I did not cry. My mother put her arm around my shoulders. "She is in heaven now," she said. "She is happy."

I shrugged her arm away and sat down in one of the kitchen chairs.

"They're like animals," the doctor was saying. He turned around suddenly and his eyes glistened in the light. "Do you know what the brute of a father was doing when I left? He was laughing! Drinking and laughing with his friends."

"There's no telling what the poor man feels," my mother said.

My father made a **deprecatory**[11] gesture. "It wasn't his daughter anyway."

"No?" the doctor said. He sounded interested.

"This is the woman's second husband," my father explained. "First one died before the girl was born, shot and hanged from a mesquite limb. He was working too close to the tracks the day the Olmito train was derailed."

"You know what?" the doctor said. "In classical times they did things better. Take Troy,[12] for instance. After they stormed the city they grabbed the babies by the heels and dashed them against the wall. That was more humane."

My father smiled. "You sound very radical. You sound just like your relative down there in Morelos."[13]

"No relative of mine," the doctor said. "I'm a **conservative**,[14] the son of a conservative, and you know that I wouldn't be here except for that little detail."

"Habit," my father said. "Pure habit, pure tradition. You're a **radical**[15] at heart."

---

[11] **deprecatory**—dismissive.

[12] Troy—ancient city conquered by the Greeks after a long war.

[13] Morelos—state in central Mexico.

[14] **conservative**—like a person who opposes change.

[15] **radical**—like a person who advocates change.

"It depends on how you define radicalism," the doctor answered. "People tend to use words too loosely. A dentist could be called a radical, I suppose. He pulls up things by the roots."

My father chuckled.

"Any bandit in Mexico nowadays can give himself a political label," the doctor went on, "and that makes him respectable. He's a leader of the people."

"Take Villa,[16] now—" my father began.

"Villa was a different type of man," the doctor broke in.

"I don't see any difference."

The doctor came over to the table and sat down. "Now look at it this way," he began, his finger in front of my father's face. My father threw back his head and laughed.

"You'd better go to bed and rest," my mother told me. "You're not completely well, you know."

So I went to bed, but I didn't go to sleep, not right away. I lay there for a long time while behind my darkened eyelids Emiliano Zapata's[17] cavalry charged down to the broad Santee, where there were grave men with **hoary**[18] hairs. I was still awake at eleven when the cold voice of the bugle went gliding in and out of the dark like something that couldn't find its way back to wherever it had been. I thought of Chonita in heaven, and I saw her in her torn and dirty dress, with a pair of bright wings attached, flying round and round like a butterfly shouting, "Give me the hammon and the beans!"

Then I cried. And whether it was the bugle, or whether it was Chonita or what, to this day I do not know. But cry I did, and I felt much better after that.

---

[16] Villa—Francisco (Pancho) Villa, Mexican bandit and revolutionary.

[17] Emiliano Zapata's—belonging to Zapata, guerrilla fighter during the Mexican Revolution (1911–1917). Dr. Zapata in the story is no relation.

[18] hoary—gray or white with age; like hoar frost.

QUESTIONS TO CONSIDER

1. What levels or classes of society are portrayed in this story?

2. What seems to most strongly influence Chonita's sense of her own identity?

3. How does the speaker's childhood differ from Chonita's? How is it similar to hers?

The sign in this window in Miami indicates the degree to which Cuba has become a part of the Floridian city. ▶

Assimilation

Cuba in Miami

COMIDAS CRIOLLAS
ENGLISH SPOKEN

▲

This market in Spanish Harlem, New York, is typical of markets found in Spain and Latin America, where there are few supermarket chains. Signs in Spanish and the promise of fresh produce attract Latino and non-Latino customers alike.

▲

As a result of the surge in Spanish-speaking populations all over the country, signs such as these have become common and necessary.

A street festival on Pennsylvania Avenue in Washington, D.C., attracts a diverse mix of Latinos, whose numbers continue to grow in the nation's capital. ▶

Before he was Bill Clinton's Secretary of Transportation, Federico Peña was mayor of Denver, Colorado. Here, he and Vice-President Gore field questions at a press conference for an airline.
▼

▲

George P. Bush waves to the crowd at the 2000 Republican National Convention, where his uncle George W. Bush accepted the party's nomination for president. George P. worked throughout the 2000 presidential campaign to help gain the support of Latinos for his uncle.

▲

Actor Jimmy Smits speaks at the 2000 Democratic National Convention, helping to rally the Latino vote for Al Gore.

▲

Singer and actress Gloria Estefan is known for being a successful entertainer and a political activist. Here, she laughs with Republican representative from Florida, Jim King.

In 2000, Elián Gonzalez, a child whose mother had died fleeing with him from Cuba, was held in Miami against his Cuban father's wishes. Estefan frequently spoke out in attempts to ensure that Elián stayed in the United States. Here she speaks to the media along with Elián's Miami relatives.

▼

MAY 24, 1999 $3.50

www.time.com

TIME

RICKY MARTIN

LATIN MUSIC GOES

POP!

▲

Moving into the Mainstream Native Puerto Rican Ricky Martin has
become a pop music sensation in recent years, selling millions of albums and
performing to sold-out audiences all over the world. He and other such
performers as Enrique Iglesias, Jennifer Lopez, and Marc Anthony, are credited
with bringing Latin music and dance into the mainstream. The image of Martin
on the cover of TIME is further proof of the Latino influence on popular
culture in the United States.

Hopscotch is published at Amherst College four times a year, serving students of Latin American Studies and others interested in Hispanic culture. The literary journal includes articles and opinions written by some of the most important Latin American, Spanish, and Latino thinkers today, as well as works by authors of years past. The journal's success is evidence of the high demand for publications that speak to the Latino community and those who study it.

▼

MOACYR SCLIAR on the art of the short story

ARIEL DORFMAN: the lost episode

GUSTAVO PÉREZ FIRMAT spells out Cuban syntax

HOPSCOTCH

Francesc Relea on Venezuela's obsession with "Miss Universe"

María Amparo Escandón reenacts the Crucifixion

Rafael Campo on the uses of poetry

Melquíades Sánchez on Vargas Llosa's libido

William Noland looks at soccer fans

Layle Silbert's photographic "I"

Ilan Stavans on novelizing the Holocaust

Plus, a dossier on Luis Palés Matos on his centenary

Volume 1
Number 2

$10 U.S. / $12 Canada

0   73361 81242   1

▲

Latino Theater Contemporary Latino theater began with the Teatro Campesino (Farmworker's Theater), founded in 1965 by Mexican-American Luis Valdez. Valdez reached Broadway with his play *Zoot Suit* (1978), shown at top, dealing with ethnic violence in Los Angeles during World War II. Other successful Latino playwrights include Cuban-American Maria Irene Fornes, who earned critical praise for her 1977 play *Fefu and Her Friends* (shown at bottom).

Fitting In

from

Borderlands

BY GLORIA ANZALDÚA

*Gloria Anzaldúa (1942–   ) was born in south Texas and moved
to west Texas as a child. She is an essayist and the editor of such
anthologies as* This Bridge Called My Back: Radical Writing by
Women of Color, *which received the Before Columbus American
Book Award, and* Making Faces/Haciendo Caras. *She has taught
at a number of institutions, including the University of Texas and
the University of California. Her interviews have been collected in
a single volume,* Interviews/Entrevistas. *In these selections from*
Borderlands/La frontera: The New Mestiza *(1987), Anzaldúa
explores the way living on a cultural border affects a person's ability
to fit in.*

How to Tame a Wild Tongue

"We're going to have to control your tongue," the dentist says, pulling out all the metal from my mouth. Silver bits plop and tinkle into the basin. My mouth is a motherlode.[1]

The dentist is cleaning out my roots. I get a whiff of the stench when I gasp. "I can't cap that tooth yet, you're still draining," he says.

"We're going to have to do something about your tongue," I hear the anger rising in his voice. My tongue keeps pushing out the wads of cotton, pushing back the drills, the long thin needles. "I've never seen anything as strong or as stubborn," he says. And I think, how do you tame a wild tongue, train it to be quiet, how do you bridle and saddle it? How do you make it lie down?

> Who is to say that robbing a people of its language is less violent than war?—*Ray Gwyn Smith*, "Moorland Is Cold Country"

I remember being caught speaking Spanish at recess—that was good for three licks on the knuckles with a sharp ruler. I remember being sent to the corner of the classroom for "talking back" to the Anglo teacher when all I was trying to do was tell her how to pronounce my name. "If you want to be American, speak 'American.' If you don't like it, go back to Mexico where you belong."

"I want you to speak English. *Pa' hallar buen trabajo tienes que saber hablar el inglés bien. Qué vale toda tu educación si todavía hablas inglés con un* 'accent,'"[2] my

---

[1] motherlode—major source of metal ore.

[2] *Pa' hallar . . . un 'accent'*—To find a good job you have to know how to speak English well. What's the value of education if you still speak English with an accent?

mother would say, mortified that I spoke English like a Mexican. At Pan American University, I and all Chicano students were required to take two speech classes. Their purpose: to get rid of our accents.

Attacks on one's form of expression with the intent to censor are a violation of the First Amendment. *El Anglo con cara de inocente nos arrancó la lengua.*[3] Wild tongues can't be tamed, they can only be cut out.

* * *

Even our own people, other Spanish speakers *nos quieren poner candados en la boca.*[4] They would hold us back with their bag of *reglas de academia.*[5]

OYÉ COMO LADRA: EL LENGUAJE DE LA FRONTERA
Quien tiene boca se equivoca.[6]—Mexican saying

"*Pocho,*[7] cultural traitor, you're speaking the **oppressor's**[8] language by speaking English, you're ruining the Spanish language," I have been accused by various Latinos and Latinas. Chicano Spanish is considered by the **purist**[9] and by most Latinos **deficient,**[10] a mutilation of Spanish.

---

[3] *El Anglo . . . la lengua*—The innocent-looking white man ripped out our tongue.

[4] *nos . . . en la boca*—want to padlock our mouths shut.

[5] *reglas de academia*—academic rules.

[6] OYÉ COMO . . . *se equivoca*—Listen how it barks: the language of the border. He who has a mouth makes mistakes.

[7] *Pocho*—Mexican from the United States.

[8] **oppressor's**—unjust authority's.

[9] **purist**—strictly observant person.

[10] **deficient**—inadequate.

But Chicano Spanish is a border tongue which developed naturally. Change, *evolución, enriquecimiento de palabras nuevas por invención o adopción*[11] have created variants of Chicano Spanish, *un nuevo lenguaje. Un lenguaje que corresponde a un modo de vivir.*[12] Chicano Spanish is not incorrect, it is a living language.

For a people who are neither Spanish nor live in a country in which Spanish is the first language; for a people who live in a country in which English is the reigning tongue but who are not Anglo; for a people who cannot entirely identify with either standard (formal, Castillian)[13] Spanish nor standard English, what **recourse**[14] is left to them but to create their own language? A language which they can connect their identity to, one capable of communicating the realities and values true to themselves—a language with terms that are neither *español ni inglés*, but both. We speak a **patois**,[15] a forked tongue, a variation of two languages.

Chicano Spanish sprang out of Chicanos' need to identify ourselves as a distinct people. We needed a language with which we could communicate with ourselves, a secret language. For some of us, language is a homeland closer than the Southwest—for many Chicanos today live in the Midwest and the East. And because we are a complex, **heterogeneous**[16] people, we speak many languages. Some of the languages we speak are:

---

[11] *evolución, . . . adopción*—evolution, enrichment of new words by invention or adoption.

[12] *un nuevo . . . modo de vivir*—a new language. A language that corresponds to a way of life.

[13] Castillian—of a region of central and northern Spain. Castillian Spanish is the standard language of Spain.

[14] **recourse**—means of achieving security.

[15] **patois**—regional speech pattern.

[16] **heterogeneous**—diverse.

1. Standard English

2. Working-class and slang English

3. Standard Spanish

4. Standard Mexican Spanish

5. North Mexican Spanish dialect

6. Chicano Spanish (Texas, New Mexico, Arizona and California have regional variations)

7. Tex-Mex

8. *Pachuco* (called *caló*)

My "home" tongues are the languages I speak with my sister and brothers, with my friends. They are the last five listed, with 6 and 7 being closest to my heart. From school, the media and job situations, I've picked up standard and working-class English. From Mamagrande Locha[17] and from reading Spanish and Mexican literature, I've picked up Standard Spanish and Standard Mexican Spanish. From *los recién llegados*,[18] Mexican immigrants, and *braceros*, I learned the North Mexican dialect. With Mexicans I'll try to speak either Standard Mexican Spanish or the North Mexican dialect. From my parents and Chicanos living in the Valley, I picked up Chicano Texas Spanish, and I speak it with my mom, younger brother (who married a Mexican and who rarely mixes Spanish with English), aunts and older relatives.

With Chicanas[19] from *Nuevo México* or *Arizona* I will speak Chicano Spanish a little, but often they don't understand what I'm saying. With most California Chicanas I speak entirely in English (unless I forget).

---

[17] Mamagrande Locha—Big Mama Locha.

[18] *los recién llegados*—newcomers.

[19] Chicanas—female Mexican-Americans. (*Chicanos* refers to males).

When I first moved to San Francisco, I'd rattle off something in Spanish, unintentionally embarrassing them. Often it is only with another Chicana *tejana* that I can talk freely.

So, if you want to really hurt me, talk badly about my language. Ethnic identity is twin skin to linguistic identity—I am my language. Until I can take pride in my language, I cannot take pride in myself. Until I can accept as legitimate Chicano Texas Spanish, Tex-Mex and all the other languages I speak, I cannot accept the legitimacy of myself. Until I am free to write bilingually and to switch codes without having always to translate, while I still have to speak English or Spanish when I would rather speak Spanglish,[20] and as long as I have to accommodate the English speakers rather than having them accommodate me, my tongue will be illegitimate.

I will no longer be made to feel ashamed of existing. I will have my voice: Indian, Spanish, white. I will have my serpent's tongue—my woman's voice, my sexual voice, my poet's voice. I will overcome the tradition of silence.

Borderlands

To live in the Borderlands means you
are neither *hispana india negra española*
ni gabacha, eres mestiza, mulata,[21] half-breed
caught in the crossfire between camps
while carrying all five races on your back
not knowing which side to turn to, run from;

---

[20] Spanglish—blend of Spanish and English.

[21] *hispana india negra española ni gabacha, eres mestiza, mulata*—Hispanic, Native American, black, Spanish nor white woman, a mix of North American and European, or white and black.

To live in the Borderlands means knowing
>   that the *india* in you, betrayed for 500 years,
>   is no longer speaking to you,
>   that *mexicanas* call you *rajetas*,[22]
>   that denying the Anglo inside you
>   is as bad as having denied the Indian or Black;

Cuando vives en la frontera[23]
>   people walk through you, the wind steals
>   your voice,
>   you're a *burra, buey*,[24] scapegoat,
>   forerunner of a new race,
>   half and half—both woman and man, neither—
>   a new gender;

To live in the Borderlands means to
>   put *chile* in the borscht,[25]
>   eat whole wheat *tortillas*,
>   speak Tex-Mex with a Brooklyn accent;
>   be stopped by *la migra*[26] at the border checkpoints;

Living in the Borderlands means you fight hard to
>   resist the gold elixer[27] beckoning from the bottle,
>   the pull of the gun barrel,
>   the rope crushing the hollow of your throat;

---

[22] *rajetas*—a coward.

[23] *Cuando vives en la frontera*—Living on the frontier.

[24] *burra, buey*—donkey, ox.

[25] put *chile* in the borscht—put a foreign spice into the soup.

[26] *la migra*—border police.

[27] elixer—elixir; sweet medicine.

In the Borderlands
    you are the battleground
    where enemies are kin to each other;
    you are at home, a stranger,
    the border disputes have been settled
    the volley of shots have shattered the truce
    you are wounded, lost in action
    dead, fighting back;

To live in the Borderlands means
    the mill with the razor white teeth wants to shred of
    your olive-red skin, crush out the kernel, your heart
    pound you pinch you roll you out
    smelling like white bread but dead;

To survive the Borderlands
    you must live *sin fronteras*[28]
    be a crossroads.

---

[28] *sin fronteras*—without borders.

QUESTIONS TO CONSIDER

1. How does Chicano Spanish help the speaker of the first selection fit in?

2. What makes it possible for a patois to develop along a border?

3. In the poem, how does history influence life in the Borderlands?

4. According to Anzaldúa, what are the advantages and disadvantages of living in the Borderlands?

The Sounds of Spanglish

BY *HOPSCOTCH* **EDITORS**

The award-winning and critically acclaimed quarterly Hopscotch:
A Cultural Review, *which serves as a forum of reflection on
arts, politics, and society, published the following piece in its 1999
inaugural issue. Spanglish became the subject of intense debate,
and, the article was reprinted frequently in Spain, the United
States, and Latin America.*

The Census Bureau has declared that by 2020 Latinos
will be the largest minority group in the United States,
surpassing blacks and Asians and numbering more than
70 million. One of every four Americans will be of
Hispanic descent. This population explosion is likely to
transform every aspect of culture and society in the
United States, not the least of which is language. In fact,
the verbal **metamorphosis**[1] is rapidly taking place

---

[1] **metamorphosis**—dramatic transformation.

already: Spanish, spoken on this continent since **Iberian**[2] explorers colonized territories in present-day Florida, New Mexico, Texas, and California, has become **ubiquitous**[3] in the last few decades. The nation's unofficial second language, it is much in evidence on 2 twenty-four-hour TV networks and more than 275 radio stations. Bilingual education has expanded knowledge of Spanish in schools nationwide. It is used in 70 percent of Latino households, and on campuses across the country it is the most studied and sought-after "foreign tongue." According to the *Miami Herald*, "Young American professionals in every field seem eager to learn it as fast as possible so as not to feel left behind."

But Spanish is not spreading in pure form north of the Rio Grande. A sign of the "Latin fever" that has swept over the United States since the mid-1980s is the astonishingly creative **amalgam**[4] spoken by people of Hispanic descent not only in major cities but in rural areas as well: neither Spanish nor English but a **hybrid**[5] known as Spanglish. The term is controversial, and so is its impact: Has Spanish **irrevocably**[6] lost its purity as a result of it? Is English becoming less "Anglicized" on the tongues of Latinos? Is Spanglish a legitimate language? Should it be endorsed by the intellectual and political establishment? Who uses it, and why? What are its prospects? The term *Spanglish* has gotten hot as the debate about the use of Ebonics (black English) has burned in schools across the United States and as the English-only movement has picked up steam.

As one might expect, these questions have contributed to an atmosphere of anxiety and fear in

---

[2] **Iberian**—Spanish, from Iberia, the peninsula that includes Spain and Portugal.

[3] **ubiquitous**—everywhere at the same time.

[4] **amalgam**—combination of diverse elements.

[5] **hybrid**—thing of mixed heritage.

[6] **irrevocably**—without a chance of changing back.

non-Hispanic **enclaves**.[7] Are we witnessing the Latinization of America? Is the nation at risk of adopting a new tongue? Is it losing its collective identity? On the other side, purists within the fractured Hispanic intelligentsia[8] refuse to endorse Spanglish as a vehicle of communication. They claim that it lacks dignity and an essence of its own. This stand is *una equivocación*,[9] though. It regards speech as stagnant, when in truth it undergoes eternal renovation. For the 28 million Hispanics north of the border, Spanish is the connection to a collective past and English the ticket to success. But Spanglish is *la fuerza del destino*,[10] a signature of unique-ness. It is not taught in the schools, but children and adolescents from coast to coast learn it on a daily basis at the best university available: life itself.

One need only think of Yiddish, used by Eastern European Jews from the thirteenth century on, to real-ize the potential of Spanglish. Yiddish was born of the disparities between high- and lowbrow segments of Jewish society in and outside the ghetto. It originated in an attempt to separate the sacred from the **secular**,[11] the intellectual from the worldly. Its linguistic sources were plentiful—Hebrew, German, and Russian, Polish, and other Slavic languages—and the mix was later reinvigorated by other linguistic additives, including Spanish in Buenos Aires, Havana, and Mexico City and Portuguese in São Paulo. At first rabbis and scholars rejected Yiddish as illegitimate. Long centuries passed before it was championed by masters like Sholem Aleichem, Isaac Leib Peretz, S. Ansky, and even Marc

---

[7] **enclaves**—areas.

[8] intelligentsia—intellectual elite; scholars and writers.

[9] *una equivocación*—an equivocation; a hedge; an intentional ambiguity.

[10] *la fuerza del destino*—the force of destiny.

[11] **secular**—things not related to religion.

Chagall,[12] whose pictorial images are but translations of his shtetl[13] background.

Obviously, the differences between Yiddish and Spanglish are many, and we are not suggesting that they have the same metabolism. Yet their similarities are striking. Latinos are already a prominent part of the American social quilt. For ivory-tower intellectuals to condemn their tongue as illegitimate seems preposterous to me. It signals the awkwardness of scholars and academics. Who are we, living in campus comfort, to require millions in East Los Angeles and Spanish Harlem to study proper Spanish? Who are we to dictate what is acceptable and what is not? As Maimonides[14] once argued, what is lofty can be said in any language, but what is mean needs a new language.

Protecting Castillian Spanish from the barbarians in the ghettoes of East Los Angeles and Spanish Harlem is futile, for Spanglish is here to stay, and it is time for the nation's intelligentsia to acknowledge it. Language, after all, changes constantly. Borges[15] wrote in an Anglicized Spanish, and Julio Cortázar[16] made his fiction come alive by writing in Spanish with a French twist. Both were condemned at various times in their careers for "polluting" the language. But who would dare to invoke Cervantes'[17] tradition now without them? Writers are, among many other things, **harbingers**[18] of change. They turn it into a testimony of their era. And rapid change is what we are witnessing in the United States today—social, political, religious, but primarily verbal change.

---

[12] Sholem Aleichem . . . Chagall—three famed writers in Yiddish and a Jewish painter.

[13] shtetl—Jewish town or village in Eastern Europe.

[14] Maimonides—Spanish-born Jewish philosopher and physician (1135–1204).

[15] Borges—Jorge Luis Borges, Argentine author (1899–1986).

[16] Julio Cortázar—Argentine author (1914–1984) who lived in France.

[17] Cervantes'—relating to Spanish author Miguel de Cervantes (1547–1616).

[18] **harbingers**—forerunners; signalers of change.

Immigrant lives are brewing in new grammatical and syntactic pots, incredible blends of inventiveness and *amor a la vida*.[19] In them binationalism, biculturalism, and bilingualism go hand in hand. Extraordinary artists and writers are translating this change into works made of words that are neither Cervantes' nor Shakespeare's but are equally legitimate.

*   *   *

What follows is a brief lexicon, selected from a pool of over ten thousand words that *Hopscotch* has begun to compile for its representativeness. . . . It is a work in progress, meant to culminate in a comprehensive dictionary of Spanglish.

—The Editors

Origins

C = Cubanism
Ch = Chicanism
CS = Cyber-Spanglish
ELA = East Los Angeles
G = General
I = Iberianism
M = Mexicanism
NE = Northeast
NR = Nuyorricanism [New York]
PR = Puerto Ricanism
SW = Southwest

n. = noun
v. = verb
adj. = adjective
exp. = expression
m. = masculine
f. = feminine

ancorman, n., m., TV news personality. [I]
anion, n., f., onion. [NR]
babay, exp., bye-bye. [G]
beis, n., m., baseball. [G]
blakou, n., m., 1. blackout. 2. blockage. [NE, PR]
bodybildin, n., m., body building. [G]

---

[19] *amor a la vida*—love of life.

chiriar, v., to use slick means to obtain something. From Eng. *cheating*. [Ch]

chiz, n., m., gossip. From Sp. *chisme*. [C]

dancin, n., m., dancing space. [NE]

drinquear, v., to drink. [C]

éjele, exp., the act of poking fun at someone. [Ch, M]

esteples, n., m., staples. [C, Ch]

fail, n., m., file. [CS]

feria, n., m., money. [Ch]

firme, exp., fine, all right. [ELA]

flipar, v., to be surprised, shocked. [NR, PR, SW]

fullear, v., to be in a hurry. [C, SW]

grocerías, n., f., groceries. [C, NR]

gué, n., m., friend. [SW]

hina, n., f., female. [ELA]

honrón, n., m., home run (baseball). [C, Ch, NR, PR]

imail, n., m., e-mail. [CS]

jefe, n., m., father, boss. [Ch, M, SW]

joselear, to steal. [Ch, SW]

kikyándola, exp., relaxing. [SW]

liftear, v., to lift. [NR, PR]

lonche, n., m., lunch. [G]

llegue, n., m., hit, punch. [Ch, M, SW]

maula, adj., m. and f., clever. [Ch]

mopa, n., f., mop. [NR, PR]

mula, n., f., money. [Ch]

nítido, adj., to one's liking. [NR, SW]

oben, n., m., oven. [Ch]

parisear, v., to hang around parties. [C, NE, NR]

partain, n., m., part-time job. [C]

piquear, v., to choose. [NE]

pocho, n., m., Mexican from the United States. [Ch, M, SW]

quire, n., m., kitten. [Ch]

quit, n., m., kid. [SW]

rentero, n., m. and f., renter. [Ch]

sochal, n., m., 1. Social Security number.
                    2. monthly check. [C]
tachar, v., to touch. [Ch]
tiquete, n., m., ticket. [G]
unión, n., f., workers' union. [G]
vate, n., f., water. [C, Ch]
virula, n., f., bicycle. [SW]
wachear, v., to watch. [Ch, SW]
wasá, exp., hello. [Ch, NR, SW]
yarda, n., backyard, patio. [NR]
yoguear, v., to jog. [C, M]
zeta, n., m., defender of the oppressed. [SW]

QUESTIONS TO CONSIDER

1. How do you think speaking Spanglish influences a person's ability to fit in?

2. What is controversial about Spanglish, and to whom is it controversial?

3. What is the *Hopscotch* editors' opinion of Spanglish?

Troubles with
Translation

BY PAT MORA AND MICHELE SERROS

Pat Mora (1942–   ) is an award-winning poet and children's book author. Her books include House of Houses, Nepantla: Essays from the Land in the Middle, Borders, *and* Agua Santa/Holy Water. *"Two Worlds" comes from* My Own True Name: New and Selected Poems for Young Adults 1984–1999, *published in 2000.*

A performance artist, Michele Serros (1968–   ) was born in La Colonia and raised in El Río, both communities of Oxnard, California. She began her writing career with stories for her children. She is the author of Chicana Falsa and Other Stories of Death, Identity, and Oxnard *(1993), from which her poem here is taken.*

Two Worlds
by Pat Mora

Bi-lingual, Bi-cultural
able to slip from "How's life"
to *"M'estan volviendo loca,"*[1]
able to sit in a paneled office
drafting memos in smooth English,
able to order in fluent Spanish
at a Mexican restaurant,
American but hyphenated,[2]
viewed by anglos as perhaps exotic,
perhaps inferior, definitely different,
viewed by Mexicans as alien
(their eyes say, "You may speak
Spanish but you're not like me")
an American to Mexicans
a Mexican to Americans
a handy token
sliding back and forth
between the fringes of both worlds
by smiling
by masking the discomfort
of being pre-judged
Bi-laterally.[3]

---

[1] *M'estan volviendo loca*—They're driving me crazy.

[2] hyphenated—connected with a hyphen, as in *Mexican-American*. Notice how Mora uses hyphens in this poem.

[3] Bi-laterally—bilaterally, having two equal sides.

Señora X No More

by Pat Mora

Straight as a nun I sit.
My fingers foolish before paper and pen
hide in my palms. I hear the slow, accented echo
      How are yu? I ahm fine. How are yu?
of the other women who clutch notebooks
and blush at their stiff lips resisting
sounds that float gracefully as
bubbles from their children's mouths.
My teacher bends over me, gently squeezes
my shoulders, the squeeze I give my sons,
hands louder than words.
She slides her arms around me:
a warm shawl, lifts my left arm
onto the cold, lined paper.
"*Señora*, don't let it slip away," she says
and opens the ugly, soap-wrinkled fingers
of my right hand with a pen like I pry open
the lips of a stubborn grandchild.
My hand cramps around the thin hardness.
"Let it breathe," says this woman who knows
my hand and tongue knot, but she guides
and I dig the tip of my pen into that white.
I carve my crooked name, and again at night
until my hand and arm are sore,
I carve my crooked name,
my name.

Mi Problema
by Michele Serros

My sincerity isn't good enough.
Eyebrows raise
when I request:
"Hable mas despacio, por favor."[4]
My skin is brown
just like theirs,
but now I'm unworthy of the color
'cause I don't speak Spanish
the way I should.
Then they laugh and talk about
mi problema
in the language I stumble over.

A white person gets encouragement,
praise,
for weak attempts at a second language.
"Maybe he wants to be brown
like us."
and that is good.

My earnest attempts
make me look bad,
dumb.
"Perhaps she wanted to be white
like THEM."
and that is bad.

---

[4] *Hable mas despacio, por favor.*—Speak more slowly, please.

I keep my flash cards hidden
a practice cassette tape
not labeled
'cause I am ashamed.
I "should know better"
they tell me
"Spanish is in your blood."

I search for S.S.L. classes,
(Spanish as a Second Language)
in college catalogs
and practice
with my grandma.
who gives me patience,
permission to learn.

And then one day,
I'll be a perfected "r" rolling
tilde[5] using Spanish speaker.
A true Mexican at last!

---

[5] tilde—mark (~) placed over the letter *n* in Spanish (ñ) to indicate special pronunciation.

QUESTIONS TO CONSIDER

1. In "Two Worlds," what is it like for the speaker to "slide" between worlds?

2. In "Señora X No More," how does it make the speaker feel to have the teacher help her write?

3. How is the experience in "Mi Problema" different from the experiences described in Mora's poems, and why do you think this is so?

Heritage

BY LORNA DEE CERVANTES

Born in the Mission District of San Francisco in 1954, Lorna Dee Cervantes is Mexican American. As a teenager, she became active in both the American Indian Movement and the Chicano Movement. Cervantes is the author of many acclaimed collections, most notably Emplumada *(1981), which won an American Book Award, and* From the Cables of Genocide: Poems on Love and Hunger *(1991). This poem comes from the anthology* A Decade of Hispanic Literature *(1982).*

Heritage
I look for you all day in the streets of Oaxaca.[1]
The children run to me, laughing,
spinning me blind and silly.
They call to me in words of another language.
My brown body searches the streets
for the dye that will color my thoughts.

---

[1] Oaxaca—city in southeastern Mexico.

But Mexico gags
"ESPUTA"[2]
on this bland pochaseed.[3]

I didn't ask to be brought up tonta![4]
My name hangs about me like a loose tooth.
Old women know my secret,
"Es la culpa de los antepasados"[5]
Blame it on the old ones.
They give me a name
that fights me.

---

[2] ESPUTA—spit.

[3] pochaseed—child of Mexicans from the United States.

[4] tonta—foolish.

[5] Es la culpa de los antepasados—It's the fault of the ancestors.

QUESTIONS TO CONSIDER

1. What does the first verse tell you about the poet's knowledge of Spanish? Why is it important?

2. What does she mean when she says "Mexico gags . . . on this bland pochaseed"?

3. In what ways does her name fight her?

4. Why is the speaker dissatisfied with her search for heritage?

Entre Lucas and Juan Mejía

BY JULIA ALVAREZ

Born in the Dominican Republic in 1950 and currently on the faculty at Middlebury College, Julia Alvarez is the author of the popular debut novel How the Garcia Girls Lost Their Accents *(1991) and other novels. Her fiction follows two patterns: an exploration of ethnic identity in books like* ¡Yo! *(1997), and a reflection on women in history in books like* In the Time of the Butterflies *(1994). In the following essay, delivered as a lecture at The Mercantile Library of New York in 1992, Alvarez offers an explanation of her personal and artistic quest.*

There's an expression in the Dominican Republic, hard to translate into English. If you ask a Dominican how he is, and he doesn't have a simple answer to give you, he might say "Entre Lucas y Juan Mejía" if he's doing well. Or, if he's doing poorly, "Entre Lucas y Juan Mejía."

"I'm fine." "I'm not feeling so good." These are straightforward responses, the black and white world of fact. And out of these two states of being, straight-forward explanations usually follow. "I'm flying high because I just won the lottery." Or, "I'm in the pits because my man left me." But in that third, in-between space, where you cannot easily get at what you feel, you need a story to **render**[1] full justice to your emotions.

Let's go back to the saying for a minute. What does it actually mean, "entre Lucas y Juan Mejía"? "Between the devil and the deep blue sea" isn't right, because you're not describing the sensation of being caught between a pair of bad alternatives—"a rock and a hard place." No. "So-so" isn't the meaning either, because the Dominican expression isn't at all meant to suggest bland stasis,[2] mediocrity. It's much more intriguing than that. "How are you doing?" "I'm between Lucas and Juan Mejía."

But who are these two guys? Who knows? The very story that inspired the saying is gone. So of course, what happens is, you have to go on and tell the tale of why you feel the way you do. What are the forces you're caught between? How did you get there? And how does it feel to be there? For me, that moment of crisis, that being-in-the-middle, is always the **nexus**[3] of a story.

So what does all this have to do with Hispanic writers living in the United States? Or rather, since I don't like to speak for all of the others, what does it have to do with me, a Dominican-American novelist?

Already that description of myself tells you something. I am a Dominican, hyphen, American. As a fiction writer, I find that the most exciting things happen in the realm of that hyphen—the place where two worlds collide or blend together. In fact, if it hadn't been for my coming to the United States at the age of ten, if I'd just grown up Dominican with no hyphen, I don't think I'd be doing what

---

[1] **render**—give.

[2] stasis—state of being at a standstill.

[3] **nexus**—core.

I'm doing today. I'm definitely not one of those born writers. I was an active little kid, not bookish,[4] not solitary in the least. Although I did always love a good story.

My parents sent me to the local American school, Carol Morgan, so I could learn my English. (That's how everyone spoke of it. It was always "your English." "You have to learn your English.") And I did a poor job of it. I flunked the subject in every grade and kept having to go to summer school. I played hookey by hiding under the bed when all the cousins would gather in the morning to be driven off to school so they could go learn their English. I wasn't interested in Dick and Jane and Spot and Puff.[5] No one could sit me down to those dull pastel puppets when, all around me, the women who cooked and cleaned—Gladys, Rosario, Altagracia y Iluminada—were full of stories about the witch that scared Juanita, who went out after dark one night and gave birth, and the baby had an extra finger. Or about the boy with warts all over his arms, Porfirio, who made Ignacio count those warts one afternoon and, next morning, Porfirio's arms were smooth as an infant's but Ignacio had twenty-seven warts on his. Or about how Fulanita was seen going into Arturo's room when Ana-Flor was out of the house and she wasn't carrying her cleaning bucket, no señor.

Those first ten years on the island, we were living in the bloody Trujillo[6] dictatorship. My father, already exiled once, was now back home and had again become involved in the underground. Our house was under constant **surveillance**.[7]

In the way of children, I didn't think anything adults did could go wrong. Then suddenly one day we were on a plane to New York, because the SIN, the secret police, were after my father. In a sense, I felt lucky. After all, I had heard

---

[4] bookish—studious.

[5] Dick and Jane and Spot and Puff—characters in a very popular series of reading textbooks of the 1930s through the 1960s.

[6] Trujillo—Rafael Leónidas Trujillo Molina, twice president of the Dominican Republic.

[7] **surveillance**—close observation.

from Rosario and Altagracia and Gladys about Nueva[8] York. Now I would get to see the miracle of the snow . . . stores full of anything you could think of to buy . . . buildings that pricked the sky with their roofs . . . and a host of other marvels that, up till then, had existed only in the province of story.

We arrived in New York City in August. Nothing I'd been told prepared me for the shock of America. I was silenced with astonishment. The doors of huge **edifices**[9] swung open when you approached them. Elevators carried you up into the sky like a ride at la féria.[10] And all around me, people were speaking English. But not the slow, carefully enunciated English of my Dominican classroom. This was **gibberish**[11]—or at best, talk I had to strain to understand. It was like finding yourself at the foot of the Tower of Babel.[12] And as the months went by, the most frightening thing of all happened. I began losing my Spanish before getting a foothold in English, I was without a language, without any way to fend for myself, without solid ground to stand on.

Determined to make myself understood, I began reading. I began studying words in a precise, self-conscious, intentional way, which is perfect training for a writer. And I began writing. In self-imposed solitude, I started making sense of my new life in this country. I discovered that the act of writing was a way of bringing together those two worlds that would often clash in my own head, driving me in different directions. A way of reconciling two cultures that mixed together in such odd combinations. At my desk, I could sort out and understand those combinations.

---

[8] Nueva—New.

[9] **edifices**—buildings.

[10] la féria—the fair.

[11] **gibberish**—nonsense language.

[12] Tower of Babel—biblical tower meant to reach heaven, whose builders had to stop when God gave them all different languages to speak, and they could no longer communicate.

I grew older and made my life here. Not here in the United States, and not allá[13] in Santo Domingo, but here in the world of words. They gave me ground to stand on as I pushed away from my family and their Old World ideas of what my role as a female should be. They gave me ground to stand on as I resisted being labeled in the New World as an "other," an outsider who had better assimilate if she expected to share in the goodies.

In a sense, I was in no man's land. No woman's land. But that land is any writer's blank page. Or as Czeslaw Milosz, the Czech poet and immigrant, once put it, language is the only homeland.

What I've discovered, then, is that this in-between place is not just one of friction and tension but one that offers unique perspectives, visions, energy, choices. And our stories chart these. And our poems name them. And this naming and charting are crucial for understanding ourselves, for validating ourselves as individuals and as members of communities that happen to be neither of one world nor another . . . that happen to be entre Lucas y Juan Mejía.

---

[13] allá—there.

QUESTIONS TO CONSIDER

1. What does "entre Lucas y Juan Mejía" mean?

2. What did the women who cooked and cleaned have to do with Alvarez's learning English?

3. Why did Alvarez finally decide she needed to learn English?

4. Why do you think Alvarez is satisfied with being a writer?

Cara de caballo

BY ALEJANDRO MORALES

A Latino literature and creative writing professor at the University of California, Irvine, Alejandro Morales (1944–   ) is a writer whose books include The Brick People, The Rag Doll Plagues, Old Faces New Wine, *and* Reto en el paraíso. *He was born in Montebello, California, and was educated at California State University and Rutgers University. This story, published in* Short Fiction by Hispanic Writers of the United States, *Nicholas Kanellos, editor (1993), puts a human face on the challenges of fitting in.*

Nowhere in the recorded histories of California is there an explanation for why Doña Arcadia Bandini married Abel Stearns. Both were from prominent families, well known and respected in Southern California. But the match of these two people was considered truly a fairy tale.

Don Juan Bandini's daughters were famous for their beauty, and the most beautiful of them all was the eldest, Arcadia Bandini. Don Juan, one of the most powerful and wealthy men of his time, believed he was destined to become a great leader. When the United States took over the northern Mexican territories, Don Juan supported the new government. He believed that California would prosper once the people accepted the new leadership, and he thought his support would one day be rewarded.

A small and dapper man, Don Juan was also highly intelligent and given to **sarcasm**[1] when matters did not go his way. He possessed one of the largest ranches in Southern California, lands which stretched from the Mexican frontier to the San Bernardino Mountains. At the height of his success, Don Juan was a ranchero whose holdings assured him a position of great respect.

Don Juan was married twice. His first wife was Doña Dolores, a lovely woman of the Estudillo family who bore him five children: three daughters, Arcadia, Isadora, and Josefa, and two sons, José María and Juanito. His second wife, Arcadia's stepmother, was Refugio, also of great beauty, from the Argüello family. Doña Refugio and Don Juan had five children: three sons, Juan de la Cruz, Alfredo and Arturo, and two daughters, Monica and Herma. Arcadia was the oldest of all his children, and Don Juan carried for her a special flame in his heart. She was born at the **zenith**[2] of his power, and she buried him in 1859 a disillusioned man.

Don Juan was respected as a man of education and of generosity, even during times of personal misfortune. He made two bad investments, the financing of a store in San Diego and a hotel in San Francisco, which forced him to seek loans to cover his family's living expenses. He went to a French gambler, poet and novelist, Leon Hennique, and asked for ten thousand dollars. Hennique gladly gave him the money, but tagged on a four percent monthly interest rate. Don Juan was

---

[1] **sarcasm**—cutting remarks.

[2] **zenith**—highest point.

confident he could repay the loan in a few months with revenue from cattle sales. But an unforeseen slump in cattle sales forced Bandini to ask Hennique for an extension on the loan. The Frenchman granted the extension but insisted on the deeds to Don Juan's homes as guarantees of payment. As the months passed, more bad luck plagued Don Juan, until he found himself trapped in an economic **labyrinth**[3] from which he could see no escape. In his panic he made more impulsive decisions, causing his business affairs to decline even further.

During this period of economic crisis, the Bandini family was constantly at odds. Doña Refugio continued to plan one expensive fiesta[4] after another, and Don Juan's sons, acting as if the money in the Bandini coffers had no end, pursued their costly gambling activities. Another kind of friction also appeared. Don Juan's sons had married Mexican women, but three of his daughters had married Anglo American men. Don Juan became convinced that the reason for his bad luck and the disharmony in his family was due to the foreign element, the *gringo* influence that had **entrenched**[5] itself in his family through his daughters. He was bitter that his daughters had chosen *gringos*, but what hurt most of all was the fact that he had encouraged those unions. He had supported the new government all the way, even delivering his virgin daughters to its men.

Now the Bandinis were on the verge of economic disaster. Charles R. Johnson, who had married the sixteen-year-old Monica, offered to advise his father-in-law. Don Juan resisted, but Johnson was finally able to convince him to sign over a temporary power of attorney.[6] Johnson then sent Don Juan and Doña Refugio to

---

[3] **labyrinth**—intricate set of paths; maze.

[4] fiesta—party.

[5] **entrenched**—fixed.

[6] power of attorney—legal right to act on someone else's behalf.

Monterrey on vacation. Arcadia remained alone with the servants on the San Diego estate.

Johnson and his brother-in-law, J. C. Couts, who was married to Isadora, reflected the Anglo attitude towards Mexican men. They considered them **incompetent**[7] and lazy. But J. C. Couts was, at least, a decent man and he finally convinced Johnson to speak with Abel Stearns about a loan for Don Juan Bandini. Johnson knew Don Juan disliked Stearns because of Stearns's hostility to Mexico and Mexicans. He also knew Don Juan and Stearns had often competed for the best *vaqueros* to work their respective ranchos. Nevertheless, Johnson decided to ignore Don Juan's feelings and he asked Stearns for a loan of four thousand dollars. Johnson described to Stearns the crisis the Bandini family was going through, and he told him that to save Don Juan's land was to save his life. Stearns agreed to inspect the Bandini holdings and consider the loan.

On the morning of April 28, 1851, Isadora and Monica arrived at the Bandini estate in San Diego to inform Arcadia that Abel Stearns was to visit that afternoon. The servants were ordered to prepare a grand feast. The two sisters then lectured Arcadia for not making herself available to men, and they advised her to make herself beautiful for Abel Stearns, who just happened to be one of the richest men in the state. Arcadia listened with half an ear. The two sisters broke off their complaints when Stearns arrived with Johnson and Couts. The three women waited on the porch of the large adobe[8] ranch home. As Stearns approached, he kept his eyes on Arcadia, not even glancing at her sisters when they were introduced. With sidelong looks of satisfaction, the two couples left Arcadia and Stearns alone on the porch.

---

[7] **incompetent**—unskilled.

[8] adobe—sun-dried brick.

Abel Stearns was born in Mexico in 1799 and came to California in 1829. He was fifty-one years old when he met Arcadia. He was the largest landowner in Southern California, and certainly one of the wealthiest. He was also one of the ugliest men in Southern California. Born a homely man, he was severely wounded in a quarrel over some wine. A deep cut ran through his nose and both lips, giving him a distinct speech **impediment**.[9] He was called *Cara de caballo*;[10] some people found it difficult to look at his face. This was the man who stood before Arcadia Bandini, a woman so beautiful that he could only gaze at her and whisper *gracias*.[11]

Arcadia stared at Stearns's grotesque face. His disfigurement forced him to breathe heavily and noisily through his deformed mouth. She noticed how large his hands were, his arms ridiculously long. But as she studied his face, she saw a kindness, a promise of a good man behind the physical distortion. Stearns asked her to marry him. He spoke of his wealth and of the things he could do for her family, for her beloved father. He promised to love her forever and to make her the happiest woman in California. Arcadia made her decision. "Abel Stearns, you are the ugliest man I have ever seen. I will marry you and I will be yours to the last moment of your life." Stearn's broken lips formed a smile. He kissed her hand and went off full of excitement to explore the Bandini estate. Arcadia called for her sisters and announced her engagement. "Send for our father and mother. Tell them I am to be married upon their return. Let the people know that Arcadia Bandini will wed Abel Stearns."

And so she did. Two days after the Bandinis returned from Monterrey, their most beautiful daughter

---

[9] **impediment**—defect; something that slows or obstructs progress.

[10] *Cara de caballo*—horseface.

[11] *gracias*—thank you.

was wed to the ugliest man in Southern California. At Arcadia's request, the private ceremony was held in the open plains of the Rancho Alamitos. The newlyweds spent their wedding night in a simple cabin atop a hill on Stearns's Rancho Laguna. The cabin was to become their favorite place, their escape from everyday life.

The years passed and the Stearnses became even more prominent members of Southern California society. To Abel's extreme disappointment, they had no children. Arcadia was relieved, because she did not want to take the chance of passing on her husband's ugly traits to innocent children. To ensure her infertility, she took special baths, ate particular herbs, and drank potions prepared for her by Indians and Mexican women. To compensate for her deliberate lack of fertility, Arcadia made love to her husband as if he were Apollo himself. Abel could hardly believe his good fortune, and he lavished the same affection on his beautiful wife. They made love with such passion and so often that Abel could not understand why they did not conceive a child. There were times when he thought he had committed a grave sin by marrying such a beautiful woman, and that God was punishing him by denying him children. Arcadia's infertility preoccupied him on his business trips, but when he was with her he forgot all their problems and let himself become engulfed by the love of this beautiful woman.

Only once did Arcadia actually tell Abel she loved him. They were in their cabin on the Rancho Laguna, and she began to think about her popularity with so many men and women. She realized it was because she was married to *Cara de caballo*, because whenever she appeared on his arm at fiestas, balls or even on the sidewalks of Los Angeles or San Francisco, her beauty was instantly exaggerated. For all that attention, for the wonderful life he had given her, Arcadia loved him very much. He was seventy years old at that time, and Arcadia was as lovely as when they had married. They made love on the braided rug in front of the fireplace, and their passion was as strong as it was twenty years before.

Abel Stearns died in San Francisco in 1871. He was seventy-two. His body was returned to Arcadia in Southern California. He of course left his entire estate to her, making her the wealthiest woman in California. When she was fifty, Arcadia Bandini de Stearns married a handsome and prosperous young man from Rhode Island, Jonathan Hawthorn Blake. Blake never asked Arcadia her age; to his eyes she was always young and beautiful. The two of them lived contentedly in their homes in Los Angeles and San Diego. They traveled extensively to the Orient and to Europe. At the turn of the century, Arcadia was as beautiful as when she was twenty. Legend has it that she was consulting a *brujo* who prescribed a potion made from ground-up brown insects. She had to drink the potion every day to conserve her beauty and her youth. Legend also has it that one day Arcadia failed to drink her potion, and the next morning her face was transformed into a *cara de caballo*. The few servants who witnessed her transformation lived only long enough to tell the story.

QUESTIONS TO CONSIDER

1. Why did Arcadia Bandini marry Abel Stearns?

2. How did this marriage affect each person's self-esteem?

3. How did the couple fit into the culture in which they lived?

Puertoricanness

BY AURORA LEVINS MORALES

The daughter of a Jewish father and a Puerto Rican mother, Aurora Levins Morales was born in 1954 in Puerto Rico. Her family moved to the United States in 1967. Morales is a writer, historian, and activist who has taught at the University of California, Berkeley, the University of Minnesota, and Pacifica Graduate Institute. The following excerpt is from an early work, Getting Home Alive *(1986), a poetry and prose conversation with her mother, Rosario Morales, about their lives as U.S. Puerto Rican women.*

It was Puerto Rico waking up inside her. Puerto Rico waking her up at 6:00 a.m., remembering the rooster that used to crow over on 59th Street and the neighbors all cursed "that damn rooster," but she loved him, waited to hear his harsh voice carving up the Oakland sky and eating it like chopped corn, so **obliviously**[1] sure of himself, crowing all alone with miles of houses around him. She was like that rooster.

---

[1] **obliviously**—forgetfully.

Often she could hear them in her dreams. Not the lone rooster of 59th Street (or some street nearby . . . she had never found the exact yard though she had tried), but the wild careening hysterical roosters of 3:00 a.m. in Bartolo, screaming at the night and screaming again at the day.

It was Puerto Rico waking up inside her, uncurling and shoving open the door she had kept neatly shut for years and years. Maybe since the first time she was an immigrant, when she refused to speak Spanish in nursery school. Certainly since the last time, when at thirteen she found herself between languages, between countries, with no land feeling at all solid under her feet. The mulberry trees of Chicago, that first summer, had looked so utterly pitiful beside her memory of flamboyan[2] and banana and. . . . No, not even the individual trees and bushes but the mass of them, the overwhelming profusion of green life that was the home of her comfort and nest of her dreams.

The door was opening. She could no longer keep her accent under lock and key. It seeped out, masquerading as **dyslexia**,[3] stuttering, halting, unable to speak the word which will surely come out in the wrong language, wearing the wrong clothes. Doesn't that girl know how to dress? Doesn't she know how to date, what to say to a professor, how to behave at a dinner table laid with silver and crystal and too many forks?

Yesterday she answered her husband's request that she listen to the whole of his thoughts before commenting by screaming. "This is how we talk. I will not wait **sedately**[4] for you to finish. Interrupt me back!" She drank pineapple juice three or four times a day. Not Lotus, just Co-op brand, but it was *piña*,[5] and it was sweet and yellow. And

---

[2] flamboyan—flowering tree native to Puerto Rico.

[3] **dyslexia**—learning disability that affects reading.

[4] **sedately**—calmly.

[5] *piña*—pineapple.

she was letting the clock slip away from her into a world of morning and afternoon and night, instead of "five-forty-one-and-twenty seconds—beep."

There were things she noticed about herself, the Puertoricanness of which she had kept hidden all these years, but which had persisted as habits, as **idiosyncrasies**[6] of her nature. The way she left a pot of food on the stove all day, eating out of it whenever hunger struck her, liking to have something ready. The way she had lacked food to offer Elena in the old days and had stamped on the desire to do so because it *was* Puerto Rican: Come, mija . . . ¿quieres café?[7] The way she was embarrassed and irritated by Ana's unannounced visits, just dropping by, keeping the country habits after a generation of city life. So unlike the cluttered datebooks of all her friends, making appointments to speak to each other on the phone days in advance. Now she yearned for that clock-lessness, for the perpetual food pots of her childhood. Even in the poorest houses a plate of white rice and brown beans with calabaza[8] or green bananas and oil.

She had told Sally that Puerto Ricans lived as if they were all in a small town still, a small town of six million spread out over tens of thousands of square miles, and that the small town that was her country needed to include Manila Avenue in Oakland now, because she was moving back into it. She would not fight the waking early anymore, or the eating all day, or the desire to let time slip between her fingers and allow her work to shape it. Work, eating, sleep, lovemaking, play—to let them shape the day instead of letting the day shape them. Since she could not right now, in the endless **bartering**[9] of a woman with two countries, bring herself to trade in

---

[6] **idiosyncrasies**—peculiarities.

[7] Come, mija . . . ¿quieres café?—Eat, darling . . . do you want some coffee?

[8] calabaza—pumpkin.

[9] **bartering**—trading without using money.

one-half of her heart for the other, exchange this loneliness for another perhaps harsher one, she would live as a Puerto Rican lives en la isla,[10] right here in north Oakland, plant the bananales and cafetales[11] of her heart around her bedroom door, sleep under the shadow of their bloom and the carving hoarseness of the roosters, wake to blue-rimmed white enamel cups of jugo de piña[12] and plates of guineo verde,[13] and heat pots of rice with bits of meat in them on the stove all day.

There was a woman in her who had never had the chance to move through this house the way she wanted to, a woman raised to be like those women of her childhood, hardworking and humorous and clear. That woman was yawning up out of sleep and into this cluttered daily routine of a Northern California writer living at the edges of Berkeley. She was taking over, putting doilies on the word processor, not bothering to make appointments, talking to the neighbors, riding miles on the bus to buy bacalao,[14] making her presence felt . . . and she was all Puerto Rican, every bit of her.

---

[10] en la isla—on the island.

[11] bananales and cafetales—banana plants and coffee plants.

[12] jugo de piña—pineapple juice.

[13] guineo verde—green bananas or plantains.

[14] bacalao—codfish.

QUESTIONS TO CONSIDER

1. What does "clocklessness" represent to the speaker?

2. In what culture would you say the speaker best "fits"?

The Jacket

BY GARY SOTO

Gary Soto was born in 1952 in Fresno, California, and attended California State University. He has received many awards and is well known for his children's books. He has an M.A. in Creative Writing from the University of California, Irvine, and taught for years at the University of California, Berkeley. This story comes from his 1986 collection called Small Faces.

My clothes have failed me. I remember the green coat that I wore in fifth and sixth grades when you either danced like a champ or pressed yourself against a greasy wall, bitter as a penny toward the happy couples.

When I needed a new jacket and my mother asked what kind I wanted, I described something like bikers wear: black leather and silver studs with enough belts to hold down a small town. We were in the kitchen, steam on the windows from her cooking. She listened so long while stirring dinner that I thought she understood for sure the kind I wanted. The next day when I got home from school, I discovered draped on my bedpost a jacket the color of day-old guacamole.[1] I threw my books on the bed and approached the jacket slowly, as if it were a stranger whose hand I had to shake. I touched the vinyl[2] sleeve, the collar, and peeked at the mustard-colored lining.

From the kitchen mother yelled that my jacket was in the closet. I closed the door to her voice and pulled at the rack of clothes in the closet, hoping the jacket on the bedpost wasn't for me but my mean brother. No luck. I gave up. From my bed, I stared at the jacket. I wanted to cry because it was so ugly and so big that I knew I'd have to wear it a long time. I was a small kid, thin as a young tree, and it would be years before I'd have a new one. I stared at the jacket, like an enemy, thinking bad things before I took off my old jacket whose sleeves climbed halfway to my elbow.

I put the big jacket on. I zipped it up and down several times, and rolled the cuffs up so they didn't cover my hands. I put my hands in the pockets and flapped the jacket like a bird's wings. I stood in front of the mirror, full face, then profile, and then looked over my shoulder as if someone had called me. I sat on the bed, stood against the bed, and combed my hair to see what I would look like doing something natural. I looked ugly. I threw it on my brother's bed and looked at it for a long time before I slipped it on and went out to the backyard, smiling a "thank you" to my mom as I passed her in the kitchen. With my hands in my pockets I kicked a ball against the fence, and then climbed it to sit looking into the alley. I hurled orange peels at the mouth of an open garbage can and when the peels were gone I watched the white puffs of my breath thin to nothing.

I jumped down, hands in my pockets, and in the backyard on my knees I teased my dog, Brownie, by

---

[1] guacamole—thick paste made with avocado.

[2] vinyl—tough, shiny plastic.

swooping my arms while making bird calls. He jumped at me and missed. He jumped again and again, until a tooth sunk deep, ripping an L-shaped tear on my left sleeve. I pushed Brownie away to study the tear as I would a cut on my arm. There was no blood, only a few loose pieces of fuzz. Damn dog, I thought, and pushed him away hard when he tried to bite again. I got up from my knees and went to my bedroom to sit with my jacket on my lap, with the lights out.

That was the first afternoon with my new jacket. The next day I wore it to sixth grade and got a D on a math quiz. During the morning recess Frankie T., the playground terrorist, pushed me to the ground and told me to stay there until recess was over. My best friend, Steve Negrete, ate an apple while looking at me, and the girls turned away to whisper on the monkey bars. The teachers were no help: they looked my way and talked about how foolish I looked in my new jacket. I saw their heads bob with laughter, their hands half-covering their mouths.

Even though it was cold, I took off the jacket during lunch and played kickball in a thin shirt, my arms feeling like braille[3] from goose bumps. But when I returned to class I slipped the jacket on and shivered until I was warm. I sat on my hands, heating them up, while my teeth chattered like a cup of crooked dice. Finally warm, I slid out of the jacket but a few minutes later put it back on when the fire bell rang. We paraded out into the yard where we, the sixth graders, walked past all the other grades to stand against the back fence. Everybody saw me. Although they didn't say out loud, "Man, that's ugly," I heard the buzz-buzz of gossip and even laughter that I knew was meant for me.

And so I went, in my guacamole jacket. So embarrassed, so hurt, I couldn't even do my homework. I received Cs on quizzes, and forgot the state capitals and

---

[3] braille—writing made up of raised dots, used by people who cannot see.

the rivers of South America, our friendly neighbor. Even the girls who had been friendly blew away like loose flowers to follow the boys in neat jackets.

I wore that thing for three years until the sleeves grew short and my forearms stuck out like the necks of turtles. All during that time no love came to me—no little dark girl in a Sunday dress she wore on Monday. At lunchtime I stayed with the ugly boys who leaned against the chainlink fence and looked around with propellers of grass spinning in our mouths. We saw girls walk by alone, saw couples, hand in hand, their heads like bookends pressing air together. We saw them and spun our propellers so fast our faces were blurs.

I blame that jacket for those bad years. I blame my mother for her bad taste and her cheap ways. It was a sad time for the heart. With a friend I spent my sixth-grade year in a tree in the alley waiting for something good to happen to me in that jacket, which had become the ugly brother who tagged along wherever I went. And it was about that time that I began to grow. My chest puffed up with muscle and, strangely, a few more ribs. Even my hands, those fleshy hammers, showed bravely through the cuffs, the fingers already hardening for the coming fights. But that L-shaped rip on the left sleeve got bigger; bits of stuffing coughed out from its wound after a hard day of play. I finally scotch-taped it closed, but in rain or cold weather the tape peeled off like a scab and more stuffing fell out until that sleeve shriveled into a palsied[4] arm. That winter the elbows began to crack and whole chunks of green began to fall off. I showed the cracks to my mother, who always seemed to be at the stove with steamed-up glasses, and she said that there were children in Mexico who would love that jacket. I told her that this was America and yelled that Debbie, my sister, didn't have a jacket like

---

[4] palsied—paralyzed.

mine. I ran outside, ready to cry, and climbed the tree by the alley to think bad thoughts and watch my breath puff white and disappear.

But whole pieces still casually flew off my jacket when I played hard, read quietly, or took vicious spelling tests at school. When it became so spotted that my brother began to call me "camouflage," I flung it over the fence into the alley. Later, however, I swiped the jacket off the ground and went inside to drape it across my lap and mope.

I was called to dinner: steam silvered my mother's glasses as she said grace; my brother and sister with their heads bowed made ugly faces at their glasses of powdered milk. I gagged too, but eagerly ate big rips of buttered tortilla that held scooped up beans. Finished, I went outside with my jacket across my arm. It was a cold sky. The faces of clouds were piled up, hurting. I climbed the fence, jumping down with a grunt. I started up the alley and soon slipped into my jacket, that green ugly brother who breathed over my shoulder that day and ever since.

QUESTIONS TO CONSIDER

1. Why does the speaker think his mother got him this jacket?

2. How did the jacket affect the speaker's ability to fit in?

3. What similarities does the jacket have to a real brother?

ACKNOWLEDGEMENTS

Texts

12 "Like Mexicans" from *Small Faces* by Gary Soto, 1986.

19 "The Latin Deli: An Ars Poetica" by Judith Ortíz Cofer is reprinted with permission from the publisher of *The American Review,* vol. 20, nos. 3 & 4 Winter/Fall (Houston: Arte Público Press-University of Houston, 1992).

22 "Peregrinación, Penitencia, Revolución" by Cesar Chavez from Aztlan: An Anthology of Mexican-American Literature, 1972.

25 "Uno" from *Bless Me, Ultima.* Copyright © Rudolfo Anaya 1974. Published in hardcover and mass market paperback by Warner Books Inc. 1994: originally published by TQS Publications. Reprinted by permission of Susan Bergholz Literary Services, New York. All rights reserved.

41 "Mrs. Vargas and the Dead Naturalist" by Kathleen Alcalá © 1992 is reprinted from the book *Mrs. Vargas and the Dead Naturalist,* by permission of the publisher (Calyx Books, 1992).

52 "Dos Patrias" by José Martí translated by Ilan Stavans from *The Hispanic Condition: Reflections on Culture & Identity in America* by Ilan Stavans. Copyright © 1995 by Ilan Stavans. Reprinted by permission of HarperCollins Publishers, Inc.

52 "Flight Out of Miami" by Pablo Medina is reprinted with permission from the publisher of *Little Havana Blues: A Cuban-American Literature Anthology* edited by Virgil Suárez and Delia Poey (Houston: Arte Público Press-University of Houston, 1996).

54 "Promised Lands" from *Chronicle of My Worst Years* by Tino Villanueva, translated by James Hoggard. Republished with permission of TriQuarterly Books, Northwestern University, permission conveyed through Copyright Clearance Center, Inc.

66 From *When I Was Puerto Rican* by Esmeralda Santiago. Copyright © 1993 by Esmeralda Santiago. Reprinted by permission of Perseus Books Publishers, a member of Perseus Books, L.L.C.

73 "Birthday" by Dagoberto Gilb, reprinted by permission of the author.

78 "Eva and Daniel" by Tomás Rivera is reprinted with permission from the publisher of *Tomás Rivera: The Complete Works,* edited by Julian Olivares (Houston: Arte Público Press-University of Houston, 1992).

85 From *The Hispanic Condition: Reflections on Culture & Identity in America* by Ilan Stavans. Copyright © 1995 by Ilan Stavans. Reprinted by permission of HarperCollins Publishers, Inc.

192 "Two Worlds" by Pat Mora is reprinted with permission from the publisher of *My Own True Name: New and Selected Poems for Young Adults* (Houston: Arte Público-University of Houston, 2000).

193 "Señora X No More" by Pat Mora is reprinted with permission from the publisher of *Communion* (Houston: Arte Público Press-University of Houston, 1991).

194 "Mi Problema" from *Chicana Falsa* by Michele Serros, pp. 31–32, 1993 (Riverhead Books).

196 "Heritage" by Lorna Dee Cervantes is reprinted with permission from the publisher of *A Decade of Hispanic Literature: An Anniversary Anthology* (Houston: Arte Público Press-University of Houston, 1982).

198 A speech to be titled "Entre Lucas and Juan Mejía" by Julia Alvarez. Copyright © 1997 by Julia Alvarez. First presented in Lawrence, Massachusetts, November 5, 1997. Reprinted by permission of Susan Bergholz Literary Services, New York. All rights reserved.

203 "Cara de caballo" by Alejandro Morales is reprinted with permission from the publisher of *The Americas Review, Vol XIV, No. 1* (Houston: Arte Público Press-University of Houston, 1986).

211 "Puertoricanness" by Aurora Levins Morales from *Getting Home Alive.* Copyright © 1986 Aurora Levins Morales and Rosario Morales. Reprinted by permission of Firebrand Books, Ithaca, New York.

214 "The Jacket" by Gary Soto from *Mexican American Literature,* edited by Charles Tatum, pp. 392–395, 1990.

Images:

Photos 58, 108, 109 *top,* **165, 166** Courtesy of the Library of Congress; **59** © Philip Gould / Corbis; **60** © Danny Lehman / Corbis; **61** © Morton Beebe / Corbis; **62** © Paul Fusco / Magnum Photos; **63** © Jeff Greenberg / PhotoEdit; **64** *top* © A. Ramey / PhotoEdit; **64** *bottom* © Craig Aurness / Corbis; **104** Ilan Stavans, 1999. Photo by Gigi Kaeser; **105** *top* © Janjapp Dekker / Used by permission of Gary Soto; **105** *bottom* © Jose Caruci / AP/Wide World Photos; **106** *top* © Miriam Berkley / Grove/Atlantic Inc.; **106** *bottom* © Roger Ressmeyer / Corbis; **107** *top* © Frank Espada / Piri Thomas; **107** *bottom* © Rick O'Quinn / University of Georgia Press; **109** *top* © Mark Richards / PhotoEdit; *bottom* © John M. Mantel/Corbis; **110** © Rafael Campo; **167** *top,* **167** *bottom* © Cindy Charles / PhotoEdit; **167** *middle* © Tony Freeman / PhotoEdit; **168** *top* © Reuters/Brendan McDermid / Archive Photos; **168** *bottom* © Dennis Cook / AP/Wide World Photos; **169** © Eric Draper / AP/Wide World Photos; **170** © David Young-Wolff / PhotoEdit; **171** *top* © Hans Deryk / AP/Wide World Photos; **171** *bottom* © Beth A. Keiser / AP/Wide World Photos.

Index